# THE END OF
# FUNDRAISING

# THE END OF
# FUNDRAISING

## RAISE MORE MONEY
## BY SELLING YOUR IMPACT

JASON SAUL

**JOSSEY-BASS**
A Wiley Imprint
www.josseybass.com

Published by Jossey-Bass
A Wiley Imprint
989 Market Street, San Francisco, CA 94103-1741—www.josseybass.com

Readers should be aware that Internet Web sites offered as citations and/or sources for further information may have changed or disappeared between the time this was written and when it is read.

Limit of Liability/Disclaimer of Warranty: While the publisher and author have used their best efforts in preparing this book, they make no representations or warranties with respect to the accuracy or completeness of the contents of this book and specifically disclaim any implied warranties of merchantability or fitness for a particular purpose. No warranty may be created or extended by sales representatives or written sales materials. The advice and strategies contained herein may not be suitable for your situation. You should consult with a professional where appropriate. Neither the publisher nor author shall be liable for any loss of profit or any other commercial damages, including but not limited to special, incidental, consequential, or other damages.

Jossey-Bass books and products are available through most bookstores. To contact Jossey-Bass directly call our Customer Care Department within the U.S. at 800-956-7739, outside the U.S. at 317-572-3986, or fax 317-572-4002.

Jossey-Bass also publishes its books in a variety of electronic formats. Some content that appears in print may not be available in electronic books.

Ronald McDonald House Charities®, RMHC®, Ronald McDonald House®, Ronald McDonald Family Room®, and Ronald McDonald Care Mobile® are all registered trademarks of McDonald's® Corporation or its affiliates and are used with permission.

**Library of Congress Cataloging-in-Publication Data**
Saul, Jason, 1969-
  The End of Fundraising : Raise More Money by Selling Your Impact / Jason Saul. — First edition.
    p. cm
  Includes index.
  ISBN 978-0-470-59707-1, 978-1-118-01005-1 (ebk), 978-1-118-01006-8 (ebk), 978-1-118-01007-5 (ebk)
  1. Fund raising.  2. Marketing.  3. Nonprofit organizations–Public relations.  I. Title.
  HV41.2.S28 2011
  658.15′224–dc22
                                                                    2010048720

Printed in the United States of America
FIRST EDITION
HB Printing   10 9 8 7 6 5 4 3 2

# Contents

*To my wife, Lisa, whose love and selfless devotion is the only reason I was able to write two books in the same year; and to my two little ones, Jonah and Max Julius, who made the ultimate in-kind donation: sacrificing precious time with their daddy to benefit the greater good.*

# Preface

Over the last fifteen years I have helped thousands of nonprofits to answer one question: How do we measure our social impact? Many—myself included—believed that if we could just prove impact, more funding would come our way. Measurement was the currency that would finally give us *leverage*. But alas, research shows that only 3 percent of donors really care about results.[1] Does that mean we should give up trying to measure? Or develop *even more* metrics? Or try to educate donors to care about performance?

No. My epiphany was that the reason we are spinning our wheels so hard is that we may, in fact, be trying to convince the wrong people.

You can create leverage only with people who *value* what you have to offer. Of course donors and foundations "value" our work from a psychic—that is, an emotive—point of view. But imagine if there were people who *really* valued our work—who *economically* benefited from the social outcomes that we produce. We wouldn't have to "beg" for contributions; we could actually "sell" our impact. We wouldn't have to traffic in the currency of psychic benefit; we could actually have leverage with rational decision makers. We could be judged not by the content of our programs, but by the quality of our outcomes. Would that such a world existed ...

But it does! Today we live in a very different world from the "independent sector" of yore. Today the mainstream economy—Wall Street, corporations, consumers, employees, and investors—has begun to embrace the value of social change. Today there is real economic currency to the outcomes we produce for education, the environment, health care, global development, even the arts and animal rights.

Still, as much as the market has embraced our work, we have yet to embrace the market. We continue to market to donors who "feel good" about our work, rather than mainstream economic actors who "value" our work. We continue to fundraise outside the walls of the economy, when we could be selling our impact within.

It is time we change. This book is about empowering nonprofits to make that change—to part the Red Sea and deliver our sector into the economic holy land.

To raise funds in today's "enlightened" economy, we must full-on embrace the fact that social change is a fundamental part of creating economic value. And we must use our energy, our creativity, and our entrepreneurialism to innovate new ways of forging social outcomes into economic currency. We will not find the answers by frittering around the edges of the economy: impact investing, venture philanthropy, low-profit limited liability corporations, and social return on investment are not going to cut it. As I write this, I am surrounded by a litter of books that purport to have the "answer"—the ultimate solution to save the nonprofit sector:

*The Power of Unreasonable People: How Social Entrepreneurs Create Markets That Change the World*

*ROI for Nonprofits: The New Key to Sustainability*

*Forces for Good: The Six Practices of High-Impact Nonprofits*

*Creating Philanthropic Capital Markets: The Deliberate Evolution*

*Billions of Drops in Millions of Buckets: Why Philanthropy Doesn't Advance Social Progress*

*The Power of Social Innovation: How Civic Entrepreneurs Ignite Community Networks for Good*

*Uncharitable: How Restraints on Nonprofits Undermine Their Potential*

*Philanthrocapitalism: How Giving Can Save the World*

The advice is thoughtful, creative, and daring. The problem is, these books are written for a different paradigm—a world in which nonprofits live outside of the economy. But we don't need to create a parallel economy: a "nonprofit stock exchange" or philanthropic capital market. The market we have is a perfectly good one. We just need to find a better way to play within it.

Specifically, this book will teach you to:

- Understand the role of social change in our economy

- Learn how to engage stakeholders

- Define your impact by outcomes, not activities

- Determine which stakeholders value your outcomes the most

- Translate your work into high-value outcomes

- Create powerful value propositions to increase your leverage

- Improve the success of your pitches to funders

This book is organized into four main sections.

*The End of Fundraising as We Know It* sets the stage for what I call the "social capital market" and describes the implications of this new economy for the way nonprofits do business. The purpose of this section is to change the fundraising paradigm and to shift our focus to a much larger source of capital than psychic donations.

*Capturing Your Impact* provides the background, concepts, and tools you will need to turn measurement into a fundraising asset. The purpose of this section is to help organizations define their outcomes and performance measures, which form the basis for your value proposition to the market.

*Marketing Your Impact* names a new set of stakeholders (called "impact buyers") who are willing to pay for social outcomes and identifies the three highest-value outcomes that these funders want to buy. This section teaches you how to create leverage by connecting your outcomes to the market.

*Selling Your Impact* will give you the core sales skills and tips you'll need to make a more effective pitch and close the deal. This section is designed to help you identify the right "buyers" and maximize leverage by communicating the right value propositions.

## Who This Book Is For

This book is aimed at nonprofits (big and small), grantmakers, corporate giving and CSR departments, government agencies, and academic institutions. It is written for executives and fundraisers, board members and funders, academics and practitioners, graduate students and undergrads, socially conscious thinkers and hard-nosed business people. This book is written to be inspiring and also supremely practical. Although the concepts are big, the insights, case studies, and tools in this book are very real, and based on years of rigorous research and field testing.

I wrote this book as a companion to my recently completed work, *Social Innovation, Inc.: 5 Strategies for Business Growth Through Social Change* (Jossey-Bass, October 2010). That book is based on a similar premise—that social change can have economic currency—and advises corporations on how to design a new generation of social strategies to create business value. Together, these books invite nonmarket and market players to push beyond what we can do with philanthropy—and to *solve* social problems by leveraging the engine of the economy.

# Introduction

## THE END OF FUNDRAISING
## AS WE KNOW IT

A food bank wanted to know how they could raise more money. "All we can show is how many meals we served," they confessed. I suggested that they focus on a "higher value" outcome—not just feeding people but registering families for SNAP/food stamps to become more economically stable. Then I asked them who valued that outcome. They struggled: Hungry families? The government? I explained that "valuing an outcome" means someone attaches economic value to it *and* has the ability to pay. I offered an idea: a large percentage of food stamps in America are spent at one store—Wal-mart. Assume your food bank can enroll 100,000 new families in the program statewide. Given that the average food stamp benefit is $133/month,[1] that's $13 million per month in new spending at retailers like Wal-mart. Now, instead of going through the back door to the Wal-Mart corporate foundation and asking for a handout, walk through the *front* door to their sales or marketing department and ask for $1 million! That's selling your impact.

It wasn't always this way. It used to be that doing good was *good enough* ...

It used to be that if you were working for a "good cause"—saving children, housing the homeless, feeding the hungry, curing cancer—donors could be rallied to support you. No one really knew whether you made a difference, and you couldn't really prove it. Still, they gave. They gave because of guilt, compassion, gratitude, tradition, religion, moral duty, personal reputation, status, peer pressure, relationships, superstition, and tax advantage. At the end of the day, giving was driven by *psychic benefits*—the feel-good factor. The only leverage we were able to create was force of emotion: compelling videos, tear-jerking anecdotes, or the personal connections between the donor and the cause. One Fortune 500 company I advised primarily supported domestic violence charities through its corporate foundation—because the wife of the CEO was really passionate about that cause. This is life in the so-called "independent sector." It is unruly, unpredictable, uncontrollable, and totally unsustainable.

For most of the economy, charity has always been an after-thought—a gesture that is made after the bills are paid, the profits are booked, and the margins are met. As a result, nonprofits have had to literally subsist off the *leftovers* of the economy: leftover money (donations) and leftover time (volunteering). Needless to say, the independent sector has been (and continues to be) a frustrating place to be a fundraiser. Because nonprofits have no real leverage with donors beyond emotion, it is nearly impossible to convince anyone that they *have to* cut a check. It is purely a discretionary, often arbitrary, volition. If a foundation or a donor decides not to award you a grant, they suffer no actual or economic consequence. It is just "nice" if they give you money.

Think about how often you've met with a program officer at a foundation who said, "This is really important work, but we're really sorry, we just can't fund your project." What could you say to convince them otherwise? The fact is, the only real leverage or influence you have is pointing out to the foundation that they face an "opportunity cost" of losing out on making a great grant. That's pretty weak. I remember one of the first times I applied for a grant for an organization I founded called The Center for What Works. We applied to a large foundation and spent months working with the program officer to write and rewrite the grant proposal, provide all of the backup documentation, and answer every question that came up. After several more months of consideration, the program officer called me and said, "Jason, we really love your organization; you're doing great work. But we just can't give you a grant; it's too risky." Too risky? It's not like they were ever going to get their money back anyway!

Here's how the Global Business Network and Monitor Institute, in their report *Cultivating Change in Philanthropy*, describes the "givens" that characterize life in the independent sector:[2]

- *Philanthropy is profoundly voluntary; by definition it is unforced.* Freedom and independence are proud features of what it means to be philanthropic, and any effort to dictate to others how they ought to give risks being rejected or simply ignored. Attempts to mandate or impose new structures and rules can constrain the creativity at the heart of much great philanthropy, or cause unintended consequences. Too many rules and requirements may simply cause some people to choose not to give.

- *Much of philanthropy is expressive rather than instrumental*— that is, the core attribute of much giving is that it expresses the values and beliefs of the institution or giver. As a consequence, an outsider's judgment that a gift is not "effective" matters less than the values it represents to the donor, the personal commitments it reflects, or the web of relationships it helps to maintain. As Harvard scholar Peter Frumkin observed to us, "At its core, [philanthropy] is about expressing values, not outcomes. Philanthropy is a vehicle of speech."

- At the individual level at least, *philanthropy is often motivated by the pleasure associated with giving* (whether that pleasure is motivated by a true desire to serve or by the personal gratification that often comes with it). To make it more "professional" or "effective" is often going to make it harder. This is the paradox of efforts to professionalize philanthropy: complexity, assessment, and evaluation require expertise and diligence, but more professionalization creates the danger of losing connection to the very personal reasons why people give. That's why professionals, used to being strategic in other domains, often behave in very different ways when it comes to their private philanthropy.

• *Endowed philanthropic organizations have little "survival anxiety"*—the anxiety that comes from sensing that if you do not improve your performance, you will be forced out of your position or out of business entirely. This idea comes from organizational theorist Edgar Schein, who observes that learning is hard because it requires giving up something you know and are comfortable with. According to Schein, the only time organizations learn is when the normal level of "learning anxiety"—the anxiety produced by having to learn something new—is trumped by "survival anxiety"—the anxiety produced upon realizing that if something doesn't change, they will not survive. Among endowed philanthropic institutions, there is almost never a threat that raises survival anxiety, which means, in turn, that there is nothing that causes philanthropic organizations to get over their learning anxiety in any consistent way. The result is a field in which there is limited (if any) feedback about donor performance, except at the pleasure of the donor, and little real need to confront and share failure.[3]

In the late 1980s, economist James Andreoni argued that the internal motives for giving were based on what he called the "warm glow" theory—people give money not just to do good (for example, to save the whales) but also to feel the "glow" that comes with being the kind of person who's helping to save the whales.[4] Andreoni's research shows that the independent sector operates primarily on a "psychic" return to donors. Or put differently, based on the current motivations and underlying dynamics of the independent sector, the primary way that nonprofits raise money is by making people feel good. And although the independent sector manages to generate a significant amount of economic activity, it is piecemeal and inherently unsustainable.

But over the last five years, something extraordinary has taken place: the market has begun to place an economic value on social outcomes. Indeed, social impact has become a valuable economic commodity: people are willing to pay for it, sacrifice for it, invest in it, and work for it. This phenomenon extends well beyond do-gooders and environmentalists to include mainstream consumers, investors, corporations, employees, and governments. Corporations alone are spending billions on environmental sustainability, social responsibility, and philanthropy. Consumers are spending more for goods and services related to health, the environment, social justice, and sustainable living. Governments are spending more than ever on education and health care, not just because they are social entitlements, but because they are affecting our nation's economic competitiveness.[5] Case in point: in 2005, Safeway spent about $1 billion on health care costs—more than the company made in profit![6]

Yesterday's social issues have become today's business issues. Consumers, employees, investors, and other economic actors have "priced" social externalities into their decision making. Here are some compelling statistics that illustrate the point:

- Eighty percent of consumers say that corporate support of causes wins their trust in that company.[7]

- Seventy-nine percent of consumers would switch brands to support a cause they care about (price and quality being equal)—and for Millennials (ages eighteen through twenty-four), it's 88 percent![8]

- Ninety-two percent of consumers have a more positive image of a company that supports a cause they care about.[9]

These trends are emblematic of a new economy—*a social capital market*—that appreciates the economic value of social change and is willing to pay for it. As you will see, this marketplace is significantly larger and more robust than the market for philanthropic or psychic benefit dollars. It's where the nonprofits of the future will need to invest their energy in order to survive and thrive.

## The Rise of the Social Capital Market

Manifestations of the social capital market are everywhere. Here are some recent stories from the *Wall Street Journal*—the bastion of hard-core business journalism—that will give you a snapshot of life in the social capital market:

- "IPO Pits Profit vs. Altruism" (*Wall Street Journal*, July 9, 2010). In August 2010, SKS Microfinance Ltd., an Indian microfinance corporation and the country's largest lender to the poor, had a glittering IPO. The offering raised $347 million in capital with a market capitalization of $1.1 billion.[10] The offering was oversubscribed by more than thirteen times the offered stocks. "The only place you can get the amount of money that is needed to help the poor is in the capital markets," Vikram Akula, founder and chairman of SKS, said in an interview. "That's why we are doing this IPO."[11]

- "For Money Managers, a Smarter Approach to Social Responsibility" (*Wall Street Journal*, November 5, 2007).

"The old strategy was simple: Avoid sin stocks. These days, it's a lot more sophisticated—and attracting the attention of mainstream firms. Changes in investing are bringing the methods of so-called socially responsible investors and those of more mainstream investors closer together. It's a trend driven by increasing sophistication among the former group, and concerns about global warming and other social issues among the latter."[12] The article also noted that Goldman Sachs Group Inc. released a report titled "GS Sustain" in which it recommended forty-four companies based on a combination of the companies' environmental, social, and governance (ESG) performance and fundamentals. Goldman argued that its picks outperformed the Morgan Stanley Capital International World Index by 25 percent over the preceding two years.[13]

- "MBAs Seek Social Change: Enterprises with a Cause Gain Ground on Campus" (*Wall Street Journal*, October 15, 2009). "This type of social entrepreneurship—that is, building a for-profit company with a social conscious [*sic*] or linked with a social cause—is becoming increasingly attractive to would-be business founders. The idea is to make money while either directly impacting consumers with its services or funneling a portion of profits to charities. Often, these companies employ people or source resources from economically depressed areas of the world that then also benefit from the charitable donations from the profits."[14] As a result, world-class business schools like Oxford, Dartmouth, and Cornell have had to create a whole new set of courses and study tracks to keep up with the student demand.

- "More Companies Conduct 'Social Audit' to Find Impact of Action" (*Wall Street Journal*, March 4, 2010). The article highlights a project undertaken by an MBA student as part of a mentorship program organized by the Center for Sustainable

Enterprise at the University of North Carolina Kenan-Flagler Business School. The program linked the student with an insurance provider that works with YMCAs, Jewish community centers, and resident camps throughout the country to conduct a "social audit." Akin to a traditional financial audit, the social audit focused on what the company is doing in the areas of the environment and ethics and its overall social impact. "It's an effort a growing number of companies are undertaking, as they look to track the outcomes of social responsibility efforts and prove their value."[15]

• "Education Contest Yields 18 Finalists" (*Wall Street Journal*, July 28, 2010). U.S. Secretary of Education Arne Duncan announced finalists in the race for federal money to help overhaul troubled schools during a speech at the National Press Club, where he called the competition part of a "quiet revolution" sweeping America to transform public education. [The program] "has unleashed an avalanche of pent-up education-reform activity," Mr. Duncan said. "It is absolutely stunning to see how much change has happened at the state and local level." Race to the Top, the centerpiece of Mr. Duncan's efforts to push innovation, aims to reward states that promote charter schools—public schools run by non-government entities—tie teacher evaluation to student performance and adopt rigorous learning standards.[16]

• "Hospitals Find Way to Make Care Cheaper—Make It Better" (*Wall Street Journal*, October 8, 2009). Be it cereal or cars, buyers usually have an idea of how good the products are and how much they cost before they buy them. That's not how U.S. health care works. Patients rarely know which hospitals offer top-quality lung or aortic surgery, and which are more likely to harm them. Hospitals don't compete on price and rarely publish measurements of their quality, if they measure it at all. Except in Pennsylvania. For two decades, a state agency has published "medical outcomes"—death and complication rates—from more than 50 types of treatments and surgery at hospitals. The state has found that publishing results can prompt hospitals to improve, and that good medical treatment is often less expensive than bad care.[17]

As these headlines illustrate, social impact now cuts across almost every dimension of our economic landscape. And what is particularly noteworthy is that it's not just that social issues are more visible, it's that they're more *valuable*. Because of this, there is greater emphasis than ever on measuring social outcomes. We cannot value what we cannot measure, as these articles well illustrate. The social capital market has also marked the advent of a new generation of stakeholders who value social change and are willing to invest in it: consumers, corporations, investors, analysts, employees, and government agencies want to buy what nonprofits have to sell. Here's a closer look at some of these new market actors.

*Consumers.* A growing segment of consumers, called "LOHAS" (lifestyles of health and sustainability) consumers, has become a powerful force in the economy. The LOHAS marketplace is described in the *LOHAS Journal* published by Natural Business Communications as "a marketplace for goods and services that appeal to consumers who value health, the environment, social justice, personal development, and sustainable living."[18] Consumers spent close to $300 billion on LOHAS products and services in 2008. These consumers integrate social outcomes into their commercial decision making, and number more than 63 million, or 30 percent of the U.S. market.[19] They are not necessarily wealthier than other Americans, but they have proven themselves willing to spend up to an astounding 20 percent premium on clean, green products over the nonsustainable alternatives.[20]

*Corporations.* Business is coming to realize that social change isn't just about compliance; it's about value creation. The social capital market is also generating new business opportunities for

companies to solve social and environmental problems. Siemens
AG drives almost 25 percent of its revenues with environment-
related products, and GE's *ecomagination* strategy generated more
than $17 billion in 2008 from eco-innovations in wind turbines,
water desalination, and other areas.[21] In many ways, the future
of business depends on social change. Companies across sectors
cannot grow without tapping into underserved "social" markets like
the uninsured, urban "food deserts," or giant developing economies
like India's. Companies cannot take advantage of these new markets
without developing "social" products and services designed to meet
underserved needs. Companies cannot hire the talent they need,
especially in developing countries, without improving educational
opportunities for young people. And companies cannot build brand
loyalty without a social or emotional bond to the customer.

*Investors.* The socially responsible investment industry is also
booming. There are 260 socially screened mutual fund products in
the United States, with assets of $201.8 billion. A total of $2.71
trillion in the United States (and about $6.8 trillion globally[22]) is
invested more broadly in various funds, pensions, trusts, and other
vehicles that use one or more of the three core socially responsible
investing (SRI) strategies—screening, shareholder advocacy, and
community investing.[23] What is most interesting, though, is that
the fastest-growing area of SRI is "community investing." Over the
past decade, community investing—putting money into underserved communities as an investment strategy—has grown an
astounding 540 percent, from $4 billion to $25.8 billion in assets.[24]
The investments earn competitive returns but also produce an
attractive social return by providing lower-income people access
to capital, credit, and training in communities that lack affordable
housing, child care, health care, and jobs that pay a living wage.[25]
Where is all this money coming from, and why? According to the
European Social Investment Forum, there are four key drivers: an
increasing demand from institutional investors, for which responsible investment becomes a matter of risk management, particularly

around the area of climate change; a further mainstreaming of environmental, social, and governance (ESG) considerations into traditional financial services; external pressure from nonprofits and the media; and a growing interest from individuals, particularly the wealthy.[26]

*Analysts.* The Dow Jones Industrial Average now has its own socially responsible twin, the Dow Jones Sustainability World Index (DJSWI), which comprises several different indices based on the top 10 percent of companies driving sustainability worldwide. The DJSWI grew over 20 percent in 2009.[27] Not to be outdone, Goldman Sachs, still one of the most venerated Wall Street firms and a survivor of the recent financial services collapse, has developed its own index called GS SUSTAIN that outperformed the market by 25 percent by incorporating ESG data.[28] Industry-wide demand for information has become so significant that Bloomberg, the leading provider of financial data, now streams ESG data on over 2,000 companies through its 250,000 data terminals. Stock market analysts increasingly rely on CSR strategies to determine the value of public companies. Researchers have shown that socially responsible firms receive more favorable recommendations in recent years relative to earlier ones, documenting a changing perception of the value of such strategies by the analysts.[29] In 2009 the Global Impacting Investing Network, or GIIN, launched as a public-private partnership supported by JP Morgan, Citigroup, USAID, and the Rockefeller Foundation, among others.[30] It's another clear indicator of the growing social capital market.

*Employees.* According to a recent survey by Kelly Services Inc., 90 percent of people surveyed said that they are more likely to work for an organization perceived as ethically and socially responsible. What's more, 53 percent of baby boomers, 48 percent of Gen Xers (ages thirty through forty-seven), and 46 percent of Gen Yers (eighteen through twenty-nine years) said they would be prepared to forgo higher pay or a promotion to work for an organization with a good reputation.[31] What's more, 72 percent of employees expect their employer to do more to support a cause or social issue (up from 52 percent in 2004).[32]

*Government.* When we think about the social capital market, governments aren't the first players that always come to mind. But they *are* players. Increasingly, the federal government and a growing number of states are looking to "purchase" outcomes through grants, competitions, and other creative funding mechanisms. According to the Obama White House, "President Obama envisions a social innovation framework for the 21st century that reflects a new social contract: citizens actively and effectively serving their communities, solving problems, and connecting their service to a larger effort. Government will serve as an innovative, efficient, transparent, and accountable catalyst for service."[33] This is the new language of government. The Social Innovation Fund, created as part of the Edward M. Kennedy Serve America Act, is part of the Obama administration's broader innovation agenda that "uses evidence to identify smart public-private partnerships" to solve pressing community needs.[34] In September of 2010, President Obama announced a groundbreaking new U.S. Global Development Policy, "putting a new emphasis on the most powerful force the world has ever known for eradicating poverty and creating opportunity ... broad-based economic growth."[35] The U.S. Department of Education has launched the Investing in Innovation Fund (i3) to invest an astounding $643 million in "innovative and evidence-based practices" that advance a set of discrete outcomes: improve K–12 achievement and close achievement gaps, decrease dropout rates, increase high school graduation rates, and improve teacher and school leader effectiveness.[36] Offices of "public-private partnership" can now be found in the departments of labor, commerce, state, and defense as well as NASA, PEPFAR, USAID, and many other government agencies.

Furthermore, social issues are increasingly becoming economic issues. In a recent survey by McKinsey & Co., CEOs were asked "Which of the following global environmental, social, and political issues are the most critical to address for the future success of your business?" Here's what they found: 50 percent of CEOs said "educational systems, talent constraints"; 44 percent said "poor public governance"; 38 percent said "climate change"; 36 percent said "making globalization's benefits accessible to the poor" [such as bottom-of-the-pyramid product development and marketing, microfinance]; 35 percent said "security of energy supply"; 12 percent said "access to clean water, sanitation"; and 8 percent said "HIV/AIDS and other public health issues." What was most amazing was that 100 percent of respondents named a social issue that was directly affecting the success of their businesses; no one wrote in, "not applicable." The very fact that McKinsey is conducting this survey says a lot about the growing importance of social issues in business. Here's a closer look at some of those issues:

- *Environment*. As a global population, we use over 320 billion kilowatt hours of energy a day, or the equivalent of twenty-two light bulbs burning for every person on the planet. Within the next century we're expected to reach a level of demand of nearly three times as much. Fossil fuels are finite, and they contribute to problems like pollution and global warming. Almost no one questions these facts now. Energy is a big problem, and big problems require big solutions. The companies that generate big solutions to the big problems—whether with wind, solar panels, hydrogen cells, or other technologies to provide alternative energy or decrease the impact of fossil fuels—are going to drive the greatest profits and the greatest environmental benefits. As noted earlier, GE is leading the way with its *ecomagination* strategy, innovating products like locomotive emissions kits (that reduce pollution associated with train operations), amorphous transformers (more efficient, lower-$CO_2$-emitting transformers used in electric grids), desalination technologies (to convert salt water to fresh water), and other energy-efficient solutions that contributed to more than $17 billion in revenues in 2008. The *ecomagination* website sums it up: "Through *ecomagination*, we're helping to solve the world's biggest environmental challenges while driving profitable growth for GE." Clearly, GE understands that social and environmental issues are potentially very profitable business issues.

• *Education*. The unfortunate reality is that most corporations are directly bearing the cost of America's education woes. Despite enormous corporate investments in education (over $500 billion annually in the United States), high school dropout rates are still unacceptably high, and the United States placed near the bottom among Organization for Economic Cooperation and Development (OECD) nations on math and science skills. As a result, companies can no longer count on the U.S. education system to produce students with the skills they need to succeed in the modern workplace. So it's not surprising that private companies are helping to create "alternative educational pathways" to foster the skills they need. Such pathways include career academies funded by corporations and private-sector apprenticeships. Higher-quality vocational schools and online learning options are also helping to address the skills gaps. Solving the education problem also presents a tremendous business opportunity for corporations. According to the Education Industry Association, education is rapidly becoming a $1 trillion industry, representing 10 percent of America's GNP and second in size only to the health care industry. Education companies alone generate more than $80 billion in annual revenues. The for-profit market includes everything from child-care and pre-kindergarten spending, testing, and training; technology; post-secondary education; and trade schools. Education, both as an issue and as an opportunity, is economically significant.

- *Health care*. The growing attention to health
care issues in the United States speaks to the centrality of this
issue to America's economy. Health care costs continue to rise
rapidly in the United States and throughout the developed
world, making this social problem even more economically
vital to solve. Total U.S. health care expenditures
are estimated to have grown from $2.39 trillion in 2008 to
$2.50 trillion in 2009. The health care market in the United
States in 2009 comprised hospital care (about $789.4 billion),
physician and clinical services ($539.1 billion), prescription
drugs ($244.8 billion), nursing home and home health ($213.6
billion), dental care ($101.9 billion), and other items totaling
$611.2 billion. America's recent passage of health care
reform legislation will, if anything, only make this industry
more attractive to business, given the government mandate
that every American be insured. With forty-six million U.S.
citizens currently uninsured, there's a big business opportunity
involved solving this problem. It's also a matter of efficiency:
38 percent of Americans, both insured and uninsured, cite
affordability of health care as the country's most significant
health care problem. These statistics point to problems but
also potential: the private sector can both address social needs
and also drive profits by innovating solutions and lowering
costs.

- *Global development*. One clear nexus of business opportunity
and social change is the increasing focus on the bottom of the
pyramid (BOP). The BOP is the world's largest but poorest
socioeconomic group: an estimated four billion people living
on less than $2 per day, in the slums of Brazil and India, the
villages of Africa, and many other places. At the same time,
the BOP's purchasing power is an estimated $5 trillion. And
by the year 2050, 85 percent of consumers are expected to live
in developing nations. Companies are well aware of this:

corporations from Starbucks to Sam's Club are setting their sights on these markets.

The increasing economic influence of social outcomes is bolstered by the fact that we are not just living through an economic downturn, we are also living through a social and environmental downturn. Things are getting worse. The poverty rate in America in 2008 (13.2 percent) was the highest poverty rate since 1997. Public high school graduation rates declined from a high of 77 percent in 1969 to 70 percent in 2000. Between 1970 and 2002, average SAT scores declined from 1049 to 1020. The percentage of workers with health insurance declined from 70 percent in 1979 to 63 percent in 2000. The number of Americans with asthma has more than doubled in the last twenty years. Childhood obesity has almost tripled, from 6 percent to 16 percent, in the last twenty years. The number of Americans in prison or on probation or parole has more than tripled, from 1.8 million in 1980 to 6.6 million in 2001. Overall, violent crime increased by 42 percent from 1970 to 2000. And that's just people. The environment isn't much better. According to a report from the Intergovernmental Panel on Climate Change, it's predicted that as soon as 2020, 75 million to 250 million people in Africa will suffer water shortages, residents of Asia's megacities will be at great risk of river and coastal flooding, Europeans can expect extensive species loss, and North Americans will experience longer and hotter heat waves and greater competition for water.[37] And NASA recently cited research showing that the number of days with record high temperatures now exceed the number of days with record cold by about a two-to-one ratio.

The exacerbation of social and environmental conditions has bolstered interest in the social capital market. Today social change is no longer exogenous to our economy. As a result, neither are nonprofits. But what does that mean? It means that the "product" that nonprofits manufacture—social impact—now has mainstream economic currency. Think about that for a minute: *Mainstream economic-actors, not just do-gooders and philanthropists, want to buy what we have to sell.* This is surely a transformational moment. Nonprofits can now transcend the world of philanthropy and become a legitimate, first-class citizen in the mainstream economy. Hallelujah!

It is this transformation that gives rise to the term *social capital market.* It's a *marketplace* in which social impact is valued, bought, and sold. The value of social outcomes is real and can be measured in dollars, not just outputs. Thanks to the social capital market, we now can tap into the *engine* of the economy, not just the *fumes.* Indeed, the social capital market literally dwarfs the size of the "philanthropic" market. To put this in perspective, let's do a quick back-of-the-envelope analysis:

*Philanthropic market.* Total size: $303.75 billion.[38] That's the total amount of charitable giving in the United States in 2009. Now take 33 percent straight off the top (for religious institutions) and you're left with approximately $202 billion.[39] That may seem like a lot of money. But then consider that there are more than 1 million nonprofits competing for those dollars, and you have an average of about $200,000 per nonprofit to work with. That's a pretty small pond.

*Social capital market.* Total size: $6 trillion-plus. Consumers are spending $290 billion annually on socially responsible goods and services.[40] Some $2.71 trillion in the United States is invested in socially responsible mutual funds, pensions, and other vehicles.[41] Governments (federal and state) are spending $543 billion on education outcomes,[42] and total health care spending in 2009 was $2.5 trillion.[43] Companies are spending a total of $32 billion on corporate social responsibility, which includes environmental sustainability, governance, risk, compliance, social responsibility, and philanthropy.[44] *That's about $6 million per organization—a lot* *more to play with.* To borrow from President George W. Bush, that not only expands the pie, it "makes the pie higher."[45]

To fully take advantage of this new market opportunity, non-profits must fundamentally rethink their fundraising playbooks and the way they do business. The way in which we raise money (such as grants and donations) today is fundamentally different from the way we'll need to raise money in the social capital market. The way we market to donors is fundamentally different from the messages we'll need to convey to social capital market players. And the kind of data we measure today is fundamentally different from the kind of data that we'll need to succeed in the social capital market. All of these things are within our reach, but they require change.

## What the Social Capital Market Means for You

> There are no market forces, there are no competitors to take market share away, there are no customers that are going to shop someplace else. The absence of competitors and customers create this kind of protected zone for philanthropy.
>
> *Tom Tierney, chairman and cofounder of the*
> *Bridgespan Group*[46]

We are in a moment of grand irony in the nonprofit sector. For the market that we once feared is now the very thing that can set us free. The price of protection from competition and customers has been our captive dependency on the whimsy of philanthropy. Now, the social capital market offers a "safe place" for nonprofits *within* the economy—a place where there is authentic demand for the outcomes we produce, not just an appreciation of the good work we do. It is this very fact—the difference between appreciation and value—that has for so long confounded the rational allocation of resources in the independent sector.

You see, in the world of philanthropy there is a substantial disconnect between supply and demand. Nonprofits "supply" social impact (social services, advocacy, and so on), but the "consumers" of that impact (that is, the beneficiaries) are often the least able to pay. As a result, philanthropy (foundations, donors, government) has stepped in to proxy the demand for these services, using their best judgment to choose which organizations should get funded and which should not.

This creates a number of fundamental problems. First, because philanthropists derive no direct value from this equation (only "feel good"), there is no market-driven desire to maximize the impact of these investments. There is, however, a moral and fiduciary desire to *minimize* the risk of these investments—ensuring that organizations are valid 501(c)(3)s, that funds are not misspent, and that nonprofits are generally competent. This "accountability" mind-set drives a reporting and measurement regime based on compliance, not performance. It's no surprise there's a paucity of meaningful social impact data about nonprofits. As one observer noted: "An individual willing to spend $300 on a digital camera can find better information than one ready to give $1 million to fight deforestation. You are much more likely to get a good answer to Canon vs. Nikon than The Nature Conservancy vs. Rainforest Action Network."[47] That's because charity watchdogs like *Charity Navigator*, *GuideStar*, and *BBB Wise Giving Alliance* are designed to respond to the needs of donors and funders, whose primary concerns relate to fiscal responsibility, compliance, and governance.

True consumers ask for different information. Imagine for a moment that you are going into a shoe store to purchase a pair of running shoes for an upcoming triathlon. You're going to ask questions like these: *Which are the best shoes? Which do other triathletes use? How much do they cost? How long do they last? Which got the best reviews?* Now, imagine that you couldn't afford to buy your own shoes, and your parents gave you $100 to buy a pair. What questions would they be likely to ask? Probably things like: *Did you actually spend the money on shoes, or did you go down the street and spend it on cigarettes? How much change do you have left over? Can I see the shoes?* Very different questions, based on very different vantage points. The fundamental difference is one of accountability versus value. Donors care about accountability. Consumers care about value. And that's precisely what is missing in the independent sector.

As we've seen, in the social capital market, social outcomes now have clear value. So what does this mean for our work? Let's review some of the high-level implications:

### 1. It's OK to Expect an Economic Return from Doing Good

Donors can use websites like Kiva.org or Microplace.com to make microloans to poor entrepreneurs and get their money back *with interest* (sometimes as high as 125 percent[48]). Companies support charities through cause-marketing campaigns and expect it will increase sales. Venture capitalists are expecting returns on companies that aim to solve the energy crisis. Toyota developed the Prius to drive profits and reduce environmental impact. General Electric is investing $6 billion in its Healthymagination initiative and projects revenues equal to two to three times the GDP.[49] Vinod Khosla, a venture capitalist who earned $117 million on his investment in SKS Microfinance, a lender to poor women in India, plans to start a venture capital fund to invest in companies that focus on the poor in India, Africa, and elsewhere, by providing services like health, energy and education.[50] In each of these instances, there is *a compelling economic motive* to solve social problems. Indeed, through creative market mechanisms like these, corporations, consumers, and investors are finding ways to value social change beyond tax incentives and psychic impact.

### 2. Donors Are Acting Like Consumers

There are over 1.4 million nonprofits in the United States, more than 500,000 of which have been created in the last ten years![51] Yet according to the Urban Institute, there are only 1,100 different "types" of nonprofit programs (such as hunger relief, after school, arts and culture, housing, elder care[52]). Simple math tells us that, on average, there are over one thousand nonprofits for each type of problem. (Yes, this is an average—there are certainly more nonprofits focused on some types of problems than on others. But you get the idea—donors have a huge range of choices competing for their charitable instincts.) That's a lot of people trying to do the same thing! There are, for example, over seven hundred charities supporting breast cancer research and prevention in the United States.[53] In effect, we have reached the point of *psychic parity*: there are hundreds of thousands of choices for where we can donate funds and get the same warm glow. Although only a small percentage of donors today—about 10 percent—use intermediaries that evaluate a wide range of nonprofits as their primary source of information,[54] this number is likely to increase.

### 3. Measurement Is No Longer Optional

Because such a high value is now being placed on solving social problems and on outcomes (not just activities), people actually need to know whether we nonprofits are really producing change or just trying to. "I don't know" becomes a very expensive proposition when people are attaching economic value to actual results. Nonprofits will no longer be able to duck the measurement question by citing the complexity of their work. Moreover, the capabilities for measuring social impact have advanced significantly, with a wide range of affordable tools, software, and classes now available within the sector.

### 4. Everyone Must Be a Social Entrepreneur

Living off of the table scraps of our economy is becoming increasingly difficult, especially when there's less on the table to begin with. Some 40 percent of participants in a 2010 GuideStar survey reported that contributions to their organizations dropped between January 1 and May 31, 2010, compared to the same period a year earlier, and another 28 percent said that contributions had stayed about the same.[55] Eight percent of respondents indicated that their organizations were in imminent danger of closing.[56] It is very difficult to control your destiny when it's in someone else's hands.

To survive, nonprofits are going to have to reclaim control of their own fate. The best way to do that is to find ways of advancing the social agenda *and* creating value in the economy. The fact is, we cannot achieve true social change today—with the reach, scale, and sustainability of outcomes that are required—without tapping into the market and leveraging mainstream economic players. Recall the earlier quote from Vikram Akula, the founder of SKS: "The only place you can get the amount of money that is needed to help the poor is in the capital markets."[57] Microfinance is clearly figuring it out. Global development is figuring it out through BOP strategies. Education is figuring it out by linking outcomes to economic competitiveness. And health care is figuring it out through linking better outcomes to lower costs. The rest of us need to figure it out, too.

## 5. New Stakeholders Have Different Expectations of Value

In the independent sector we used to get by with just doing good work and using pictures and anecdotes to tell our story. But in the social capital market there is a new set of actors who are placing huge economic bets on the value we can create—and picture and stories won't cut it. Moreover, these folks aren't just looking for "reach" or "raised awareness"; they're looking to *solve* social problems. So we need to figure out how to capture, market, and sell high-value outcomes—the outcomes most relevant to actually solving those problems. Bottom line: Now that there are direct economic consequences of social change, the margin for error (and failure) is that much narrower. Performance (and results) needs to be that much greater.

### 6. Higher Expectations of Value Require Greater Innovation

To actually *solve* social problems, nonprofits will need to go beyond programs and initiatives and come up with more entrepreneurial, innovative, and systemic approaches to solving problems. This means that we can't just keep doing what we're doing and hope that someone will fund it. If people are really buying impact, not just funding programs, then we need to innovate better strategies to produce those impacts. That requires a whole new playbook: public-private partnerships, new technologies, new incentives and mechanisms, more cutting-edge theories of change, and so on.

The social capital market portends a whole new way of doing business in the nonprofit sector, a whole new way of fundraising, and a whole new way of thinking about impact. It is exciting, daunting, and revivifying. But although the social capital market means many things for nonprofits, there are also many things that it does *not* mean. Let's consider a few of these.

### It's Not About Making Nonprofits Run Like Businesses

This is not about bringing the business world (and business think-ing) into the nonprofit sector; *it's about bringing the nonprofit sector into the business world.* Although there are certainly many benefits nonprofits can derive from better management skills, new business models, and more focus on results, being more "businesslike" will not help nonprofits raise more money or even generate better results. Moreover, if anything, the social capital market means that we need nonprofits to keep doing exactly what they're doing: creating positive social change. We just need to find better ways of connecting those efforts to the economy.

### It's Not About Changing Foundation and Donor Behavior

Nonprofit thought leaders and academics have called for increased efforts to "educate" donors to ask for better information, make more rational decisions, and invest more resources in high-performing nonprofits. But trying to make psychic investors more rational—that is, to change their motivations, or to get them to value different things about nonprofits—is *not* the solution. And that isn't what the social capital market is about. Rather, it's about tapping into a new class of investors—investors who value the outcomes that nonprofits produce *and are willing to pay for them,* because those outcomes produce direct benefits to those investors.

## It's Not About "Social Return on Investment"

There is a difference between *value* and *measurement.* Value is quantified by the direct benefits to stakeholders that are produced by social change. For example, the value to McDonald's of Ronald McDonald House Charities (RMHC) is clear:

> At McDonald's, the support of RMHC is also critical to the success of business, as it helps build vital trust between customers and the brand. Research shows that 92 percent of Americans have a more positive image of companies that support a cause. And, 87 percent of Americans are likely to switch brands, when price and quality are equal, to support a cause. These trends are consistent around the globe. Having a brand that openly values and supports important causes—and takes purposeful steps to engage customers who have those same values—is one of McDonald's key goals.[58]

(You'll learn more about RMHC in the course of this book, because the organization artfully straddles both the philanthropic and social capital markets.)

The social capital market doesn't require us to come up with newfangled ways to conjure up a "social return" number that is academic or notional. Calculations such as "social return on investment" (SROI) were originally designed to "measure the societal benefit created by a social purpose enterprise."[59] SROI metrics include "tracking social outcomes of ordinarily difficult to monetize measures of social value, such as increases in self-esteem and social support systems, or improvements in housing stability."[60] These types of metrics and related "social impact measurement" efforts are noble and worthy, but they aim to satisfy a different set of stakeholders (primarily philanthropists) than the customers we serve in the social capital market. If anything, measurement in the social capital market is much easier, because people know exactly what they want (and what they value).

## It's Not About Creating a "Philanthropic Capital Market"

Many in the social sector have long pined for a true "market" for social impact. With great enthusiasm and creativity, thought leaders, academics, social entrepreneurs, and enlightened MBA do-gooders have Mister-Potato-Headed together just about every permutation of "philanthropy" and "capital" that you could imagine, positing nonprofit investment banks, philanthropic capital markets, social stock exchanges, philanthrocapitalism, social impact investing, social venture capital funds, social business, venture philanthropy, and more. But these concepts are all just more businesslike ways of conducting philanthropy. At the end of the day, they are still predicated on giving away money (or subsidizing it), not on maximizing value creation. The social capital market is about identifying the economic value in social change and finding ways to use *existing* market forces to discover that value.

This simple fact is that social change has a legitimate place in our economy. This fact is renewing our faith in markets, and it's also renewing our faith in nonprofits. This book provides the formula for how nonprofits can thrive in today's social capital market.

We'll begin the work in Part One, which will show you how to capture your impact.

# Part I

## CAPTURING YOUR IMPACT

### From "What" to "So What?"

**Key Takeaways**

- Know your inventory

- Measure outcomes, not activities

- Make sure it's about contribution, not attribution

- Develop your own Success Equation

Here's the good news: someone wants to buy what you have. Now here's the problem: most of us don't really know what we have to sell! These next few chapters will teach you how to capture the impact of your day-to-day activities and translate that impact into powerful value propositions that the market can relate to.

I'll never forget the person who first taught me how to sell. His name was Bill Kowalski, and he was a million-dollar salesman—of men's suits. On my first day of work, Bill told me that I wasn't allowed to talk to any customers. All he wanted me to do was try on clothes—in fact, I was to try on every single suit in the store. My assignment was to learn which suits fit snug, which were loose; which are cut for older men, which weren't; which have a six-inch drop and which have an eight-inch drop; how many we had in

27

each size and how many we had at every price point. At the end of the week, Bill told me the point of this seemingly pointless exercise: "The fact is that 90 percent of the sale is made before the customer ever walks through the door! You gotta know your inventory. The minute the customer comes in, you have to be able to size him up, figure out what he's looking for, and know exactly what you have in stock that can meet his needs."

Although selling suits may be a far cry from saving lives, the principle is the same: before you can sell anything, *you gotta know your inventory*. But what exactly do nonprofit organizations have to sell? Typically, we sell the feel-good factor—psychic benefits that people experience from knowing that they are supporting a good cause. There's nothing wrong with that; we do important work, and it does feel good. But behind all the pictures, the stories, and the mission statements lies the essence of what we're really selling: the *outcomes* we produce. The outcomes are the positive changes in the world that we create as a result of the work we do: the lives we change, the jobs we create, the awareness we raise, the skills we teach, the animals we save, the land we protect, and the children we inoculate.

There are a number of reasons why nonprofits struggle with capturing their impact. First, nonprofit organizations commonly focus more on the "what" than the "so what." We typically identify our organizations by our activities: research, counseling, the arts, education, job training, helping kids with disabilities. Sometimes, we lose the "so what" altogether! I'll never forget a conversation I had with an executive director of an arts organization about joining her board. She told me how it was a real priority for her organization to engage young artists, as most of their members were older, more established artists. And then she slid a stack of newspapers across the table for me to review: "This is our flagship; we spend 80 percent of our budget on this newspaper," she boasted. Then I asked the obvious "so what" question: "How many young artists do you reach through this paper?" "None," she said. "They're all on the Web!" So why did the organization continue to publish this costly paper? The response: "We've always had that newspaper!" Hers was no different from most nonprofits, which define themselves by their programs (what they do), not their outcomes (the change they create).

We know so little about our impact in part because measurement can be complicated. For many nonprofits, it could take years to determine whether their programs were ultimately successful. Did the trainee get a job and keep it? Did the student graduate? Did the woman in an abusive relationship become financially self-sufficient? Were the endangered species saved? Did human rights abuses lessen in that region of the world? Did the at-risk children avoid a life of gang violence and drugs?

It's hard to know the answers to any of these questions. And it's even harder to prove. Outcomes often unfurl over time, and the longer it takes, the more variables there are that can confuse the analysis: changing economic conditions, different public policy, emerging social influences, media attention to an issue, even the weather! Without spending a small fortune, few of us will ever be able to prove that our programs produced certain long-term effects.

Another reason we don't know our impact is that many nonprofit organizations tend to have an ethos or culture that values preservation over performance. On one level this is structural: most budgets are built around programs, not outcomes. Funders give grants for programs, not outcomes. People develop their competencies around programs, not outcomes. The program-centric mentality is designed to preserve a nonprofit's activities at all costs—even if they don't work! But there's another reason why the culture doesn't value "knowing" about impact: people don't believe it's possible, so they don't even bother. Many nonprofits end up in this circular loop of not measuring impact because they don't think it's possible and then not thinking it's possible because they've never tried to measure!

Finally, organizations don't measure results because there is little incentive to do so. Measurement has been imposed by funders as a compliance requirement. At best, nonprofits can comply with grant requirements and fulfill the expectations that got them the money in the first place. At worst, it's a huge pain in the rear. In neither case is there any upside. If there was some more organic, market-driven incentive, nonprofit managers would measure on their own volition. The rewards for measurement do not sufficiently outweigh the costs—whether psychological (such as fear of failure or penalties) or actual (such as hiring evaluators).

A few years back I was advising a large community foundation on how to measure the impact of their grants. One grant in particular stood out from the rest: it was the foundation's largest commitment—$1 million per year—and was awarded to a youth violence prevention program. The grant was up for its annual renewal, and the board pressed for more than a perfunctory annual report—they wanted to know if the grant was making any real impact on gang violence. The program officer protested, arguing that it would take ten to fifteen years to determine whether or not the youth would end up on the streets. The board insisted that there must be some information that could answer whether or not their grant was making a difference. Still, the program officer demurred, claiming that impact would take years to measure, and even then, no one would know for sure if the program worked. So guess how much money the organization was awarded that year? You got it: zero.

Some are even beginning to question the very existence of charities. As the number of new nonprofits continues to grow at metastatic rates—46,633 new 501(c)(3) organizations created in 2009, and between 40,000 and 50,000 in 2007 and 2008[1]—some in Congress are questioning whether all of these nonprofits are really necessary. "Especially during these tough economic times, it's troubling to hear we are increasing the number of these organizations at such a rapid pace," said Representative Xavier Becerra, a California Democrat who closely follows the nonprofit sector.[2] "It's not free," Mr. Becerra said, "and so we need to do something to make sure taxpayers are getting a big enough benefit in return."[3] Here's a fascinating statistic: the $300 billion donated to charities in 2009 cost the federal government more than $50 billion in lost tax revenue.[4]

While some are questioning the value of charities, others are paying a premium for that value. And that's the power of the social capital market: it flips the presumption of value about nonprofits. It is not focused on *justifying* that nonprofits are worthy or *proving* that nonprofits create some value; rather, the social capital market is based on "value"—financing the outcomes that nonprofits can produce. The social capital market also gives us a new set of incentives to measure—not because we *have to*, but because we realize that outcomes are the currency of this new market and what will give us *real* leverage to attract funding. That's a whole new world, and an exciting one!

To succeed in this new market, we'll need to be clear on what "outcomes" really mean, which outcomes we can produce, and how to measure our contribution to those outcomes. These next few chapters will teach you how.

In Chapter One, you'll learn about the important shift from demonstrating accountability (*we did what we said we would*) to showing value (*our outcomes are worth your investment*).

In Chapter Two, you'll learn about the differences between evaluation and measurement, outcomes and activities, and good measures and bad measures.

And in Chapter Three, you'll see how to combine what you've learned in the previous two chapters into a simple Success Equation so that you can capture and communicate your true impact.

# Chapter 1

# FROM ACCOUNTABILITY TO VALUE

Google the word "evaluation" and you'll get over a hundred million results in less than a minute.[1] There are hundreds of different approaches, and most are confoundingly complex. Indeed, measuring impact is the elusive holy grail of the nonprofit sector. And lately there seem to be a cavalcade of white knights hoping to save the sector. Journalists, bloggers, armchair evaluators, foundation CEOs, and self-styled philanthropic "analysts" pontificate solipsistically about logic models, theories of change, "Morningstar-like" rating services, sector-wide taxonomies, Zagat guides, and philanthropic "data management systems." It's all so audacious! Unfortunately, everyone seems to be blindly whacking away at the piñata of measurement without even knowing what's inside. And that's the bigger problem: it's not that we can't figure out the answer—it's that we're not really sure what we're asking for.

There's a lot at stake in getting this right. If we want to be able to *sell* our impact in the social capital market, we first have to *know* our impact. And in order to know our impact, and communicate it in some compelling way, we need to be able to quantify or measure it. This chapter explores the different drivers for measuring impact, explains the basic concepts, and introduces a simple framework that organizations can use to best capture and communicate their value.

## Impact as Accountability

In the independent sector, our notions of impact are heavily influenced by individual donors, government, and foundations (those who support our work financially). There is of course an inherent mission-driven urge to improve our impact, but in my experience this is seldom the true driver of organizational desire to measure results. Case in point: I remember when I first started teaching classes for nonprofit executives at Northwestern University's Kellogg School of Management. It was 2004, and I had just released my first book, *Benchmarking for Nonprofits*. My first course was aptly titled "Benchmarking for Nonprofits: How to Measure and Improve Your Impact." I think maybe ten or twelve organizations signed up for the class; that was barely enough to keep it in the curriculum. The class went well, but the marketing team at Kellogg had a suggestion: "Why don't we change the name for the next offering?" They renamed it: "Performance Counts: How to Raise More Money by Demonstrating Results." Wouldn't you know, the class was packed!

How we think about measurement today is very much informed by the mentality of the independent sector, where donors consider themselves benefactors and nonprofits consider themselves the beneficiaries of largesse. This system of thinking has cultivated an "accountability" mind-set, wherein measurement is primarily used to account for financial resources and prove that donations were not misspent. Even when nonprofits seek to prove their effectiveness on a more rigorous basis, it is often to reassure donors that their dollars won't be wasted. According to the National Council of Nonprofits, "Two aspects of ethical practice have been most prominent in shaping the recognized 'best practices' of nonprofit organizations: accountability and transparency."[2] In a world of accountability, "best practices" are really just outstanding ways of proving that you're not bad. If the *best* we can do is not to be our worst, we may in fact have set the bar too low. This mentality is being driven by two forces: a heavily fortified legal regime and donor intent.

Over the years, a significant ethics and legal infrastructure has been created to guard against financial mismanagement, conflicts of interest, and tax code violations among nonprofits. An endless stream of high-profile scandals involving misappropriation of funds, fraud, and excessive compensation—most notably the one involving United Way in 1992—have only built up more legislative scar tissue. These developments have been a major factor in influencing the way we think about measurement today. Here are the major primogenitors of today's accountability regime:

- *IRS Form 990*. Form 990 is the Internal Revenue Service's primary tool for gathering information about tax-exempt organizations, for educating organizations about tax law requirements, and for promoting compliance with tax law.[3] It was primarily designed for monitoring and disclosure, not for setting performance standards for nonprofits. Form 990 has been the dominant source of information about nonprofits to date, serving up the majority of data made available to donors on such websites as Guidestar and Charity Navigator. The 990 does have a section (Part III) focused on "Service Efforts and Accomplishments" that requires organizations to list the accomplishments for their three largest (by expense) program services. Specifically, the IRS requires that organizations describe "program service accomplishments through specific measurements such as clients served, days of care provided, number of sessions or events held, or publications issued."[4] The 990 also requires "the activity's objective" both short-term and long-term.[5] This is the closest thing to any mandatory performance reporting for nonprofits, but this information has not been standardized in any way by the IRS, and most nonprofits report narrative data that is difficult to aggregate or analyze. The 990 also requires information about accountability and transparency, such as the composition of the board of directors, and answers to questions regarding conflict of interest policies, procedures for managing conflicts, a whistleblower protection policy, and a document retention policy.[6]

• *Sarbanes-Oxley Act of 2002.* One of the most influential laws affecting nonprofit accountability is the Sarbanes-Oxley Act of 2002, which was passed in the wake of the Enron scandal and created significant accountability requirements for publicly traded companies. Two of its provisions also applied to nonprofits: (1) a prohibition against destruction of documents that are tied to a criminal investigation, and (2) a prohibition of retaliation against whistleblowers. Though much of the Act is focused on public companies, many nonprofit boards have still benchmarked their accountability practices against the requirements of this Act as a precautionary measure.

• *The California legislature's passage of the Nonprofit Integrity Act.* In 2004, Governor Schwarzenegger approved the Nonprofit Integrity Act, which establishes certain accountability requirements for nonprofits operating in California. The Act requires audits for nonprofits above a certain size and mandatory board review of compensation for the CEO and CFO. It also regulates fundraising practices and prohibits various fraudulent or misleading fundraising practices.

In addition to these laws, many voluntary ethical codes and "accountability standards" have been promulgated. The Maryland Association of Nonprofit Organizations, for example, has created a set of fifty-five standards for nonprofits and a companion "Seal of Excellence" that organizations can apply for and license.

The standards are based on "fundamental values—such as honesty, integrity, fairness, respect, trust, compassion, responsibility, and accountability" and describe how nonprofits should act to be ethical and be accountable in their program operations, governance, human resources, financial management, and fundraising.[7]

Donor expectations further reinforce this accountability mentality. When it comes to measurement and data, most donors are primarily interested in this information to avoid making investments in "bad" charities, as opposed to informing their choices about which are the best ones. A recent survey (May 2010) by UK-based polling company YouGov reveals that over two-thirds of the British public (68 percent) would transfer their donations away from a charity if it were found to be performing badly. But only 18 percent claim they would feel more obliged to give to a charity they knew was performing well.[8] That pretty much sums it up.

In 2010, Hope Consulting completed a widely respected study called *Money for Good* in order to "understand US consumer preferences, behaviors, and demand for impact investment products and charitable giving opportunities."[9] The research focused on the largest segment of donors: those with household incomes over $80,000 (representing 75 percent of the charitable contributions from individuals) and focused specifically on high net-worth individuals, with incomes in excess of $300,000.[10] The findings support an accountability-type mind-set. Here's what they found:

- For better or for worse, Overhead Ratio is the number-one piece of information donors are looking for.

- In general, people are looking for comfort that their money will not be "wasted" (top three answers)

- Although donors say they care about nonprofit performance, very few actively donate to the highest-performing nonprofits, and very few spend any time looking into it.

- Donor comments:
  - "I look at what percentage of dollars actually goes to those being helped. I will look that up if it is easy to find."
  - "I look for 25 percent or lower admin costs."
  - "It's too hard to measure social impact."
  - "I'm not a mini-foundation; don't treat me like one."

- For the 35 percent of donors who do perform research, it is often to "validate" their choice of charity:
  - "I just want to make sure my charities 'hurdle the bar'; I don't care by how much."
  - "I just want to ensure that I'm not throwing my money away."
  - "I can't determine which is the 'best' nonprofit, but I can find out if a nonprofit is bad."
  - "We give to faith-based organizations if they are accredited by our church."

- Eighty-five percent of people say they do care about nonprofit performance, but only 3 percent make donations based on relative performance.

- Changing these donors behaviors will be challenging, due in large part to three critical barriers:
  - Donors don't give to "maximize impact" ("I give because it makes me feel good").
  - There is no "burning platform" to motivate change ("I don't research, but I am sure that the nonprofits to which I donate are doing a great job").
  - Donors are loyal. ("I give to the same organizations each year. Some metric won't change that.")

The lessons are pretty clear: the vast majority of philanthropic donors are *not* looking to make their giving decisions based on an organization's outcomes or performance. Most donors want to make sure nonprofits are well run and aimed at a problem they care about. The report concluded: "In general, people are looking for comfort that their money will not be 'wasted.'"

Most of the donor information and nonprofit watchdog sites are similarly inclined. They also reinforce the message to nonprofits that the way to communicate your impact to prospective funders is by demonstrating accountability. Following are some representative samples.

### Charity Navigator

This organization calls itself "America's premier independent charity evaluator" and has analyzed the "financial health" of over 5,500 nonprofits. According to Charity Navigator, "We rate charities by evaluating two broad areas of financial health, their organizational efficiency and their organizational capacity."[11]

- *Organizational efficiency.* Analyzing a charity's efficiency reveals how well it functions day to day. Charities that are efficient spend less money to raise more. Their fundraising efforts stay in line with the scope of the programs and services they provide. They keep administrative costs within reasonable limits. They devote the majority of their spending to the programs and services they exist to provide. Charity Navigator analyzes four performance categories of organizational efficiency: program expenses, administrative expenses, fundraising expenses, and fundraising efficiency.[12]

- *Organizational capacity.* We analyze a charity's capacity to determine how well it has sustained its programs and services over time, and whether it can continue to do so, even if it loses support or faces broad economic downturns. By doing so, we show givers how well that charity is positioned to pursue long-term, systemic change. Charities that show consistent growth and maintain financial stability are more likely to last for years to come. They have the financial flexibility to plan strategically and pursue long-term objectives, rather than facing flurries of fundraising to meet payrolls and other short-term financial obligations. These charities can more ambitiously address our nation's challenges, envisioning and working toward long-term solutions. Charity Navigator analyzes three categories of organizational capacity: primary revenue growth, program expenses growth, and working capital ratio. We issue a score in each category, as well as a rating that combines a charity's performance in all three categories.[13]

## The BBB Wise Giving Alliance

This intermediary evaluates 501(c)(3) organizations on four dimensions: how they govern, how they spend money, the truthfulness of their representations, and their willingness to disclose basic information. BBB rates nonprofits on the following four "accountability" standards:

- *Governance and oversight:* The governing board has the ultimate oversight authority for any charitable organization. This section of the standards seeks to ensure that the volunteer board is active, independent, and free of self-dealing.[14]

- *Measuring effectiveness:* An organization should regularly assess its effectiveness in achieving its mission. This section seeks to ensure that an organization has defined, measurable goals and objectives in place and a defined process in place to evaluate the success and impact of its program(s) in fulfilling the goals and objectives of the organization and that also identifies ways to address any deficiencies.[15]

- *Finances:* This section of the standards seeks to ensure that the charity spends its funds honestly, prudently, and in accordance with statements made in fundraising appeals.[16]

- *Fundraising and informational materials:* A fundraising appeal is often the only contact a donor has with a charity and may be the sole impetus for giving. This section of the standards seeks to ensure that a charity's representations to the public are accurate, complete, and respectful.[17]

All of this information may help a donor weed out bad apples, but it's unlikely to provide much information to help a donor decide whether a nonprofit is creating any significant social impact or which of many organizations is producing the best results.

## Givewell

This donor ratings service purports to be more focused on effectiveness, claiming: "Unlike existing evaluators, which focus solely on financials, assessing administrative or fundraising costs, we focus on how well programs actually work—i.e., their effects on the people they serve."[18] Givewell uses four key criteria to help donors analyze and pick charities:

- Is there evidence that a charity's programs are effective?

- Are a charity's programs cost-effective?

- Can the charity productively use additional funds?

- Is the above information shared transparently?

Givewell's rigorous focus on evaluation certainly sets it apart from other donor sites, but its primary focus is accountability. Nonprofits are evaluated or measured not on their level of performance, but rather on absolute effectiveness (that is, whether it works *at all)* and on the organization's commitment to evaluation. Here is an excerpt from one of Givewell's analyses, this one pertaining to "developing world education":

> Our top recommendation in this cause is Pratham. Pratham has, in the past, shown a commitment to rigorous evaluation of its programming. This commitment does not by itself answer all the questions above, but to us it implies an organizational commitment to learning about what works and holding itself accountable. This charity has been closely involved with some of the studies discussed below and has completed a number of projects that have been evaluated by the Poverty Action Lab at M.I.T.[19]

The spotlight and focus on accountability from these nonprofit ratings websites puts pressure on nonprofits to think about their impact in a certain way: as a matter of compliance and donor risk aversion.

This accountability mentality is structurally reinforced through the ways in which donors give money. It helps to explain why so many foundations insist on "restricted" grants as opposed to letting nonprofits use funds for "general operating" purposes: general operating funds are harder to account for and could be construed to be "wasted" on overhead. (Grants to *general operating funds* can be used for any purpose the nonprofit wishes; *restricted grants* can be used only for the purpose designated by the grantmaker.) Accountability and risk management is usually behind another form of funding: grants commonly referred to as "challenge" grants (*we will give this much, but only if you raise this much first*). And accountability also explains the whole complex reporting regime in place for most government and foundation grants—few of which ever get read or used in any meaningful way.

All of these accountability drivers have created a due diligence "regime" that relegates measurement to the purpose of reassuring donors and proving that nonprofits are worthy of investment. In effect, measurement has become a kind of insurance policy for the donor. The current approach to measurement focuses on two primary questions:

1. *Did you do what you said you were going to do?* And did you use resources responsibly and account for them? This information is primarily designed to satisfy funder requirements and compliance reporting requirements.

2. *How can you prove that your program works?* And what type of research and evidence do you have to back this up? This information is primarily designed to establish credibility and trust with donors.

Measuring impact for accountability is particularly challenging for nonprofits because there are no common standards for what to measure. Beyond controlling risk (of losing money), it's often unclear what psychic benefit donors really want to know. What does it take to be "accountable" or to *prove* that you are "effective"? There are endless numbers of frameworks, methodologies, standards, calculations, rubrics, and measurement systems. As a result, nonprofits often end up mired in confusion or overcompensate by chasing their tails, measuring everything they can think of.

One reason donor interest in nonprofit performance data is so inchoate is that the primary value of a donor's gift—the psychic impact or "warm glow" of making the gift—is realized at the time the gift is made. Research supports this point: a ground-breaking study published in the journal *Science* found that when people made a decision to voluntarily donate money to charity, they experienced a burst of increased neural activity and heightened satisfaction in areas linked to reward processing at the moment of the decision.[20] The research described the effect as "associated with neural activation similar to that which comes from receiving money for oneself."[21] Because the primary intent of most donors is emotional, and the primary value of that psychic benefit is realized up front, any post-hoc data regarding a nonprofit's impact, although interesting, has no particular value or utility to donors.

This accountability approach to measurement has limited value to nonprofits in a social capital market, where stakeholders are less concerned about wasting money and more concerned about purchasing social outcomes that have value to them. Accountability is not the benchmark in the social capital market, it's just the price of entry. To succeed, nonprofits need to embrace a new approach to measurement, one that shifts the focus from compliance and accountability to value creation.

## Impact as Value

The social capital market has created a different reason for nonprofits to measure impact: it's not about counting, it's about convincing. In this new market, nonprofits are motivated to measure their impact to demonstrate "value" created for existing stakeholders and to *influence* the resource allocation decisions of prospective stakeholders. Measuring impact in this way is about demonstrating that a nonprofit is making a meaningful contribution to outcomes—both social and economic—that stakeholders highly value. Measurement enables you to quantify and communicate the *degree* of value (such as outcomes) created by the work you are doing. If a particular stakeholder—a government agency or a corporation—*really* values the outcome, they're going to want to know how much impact was produced, not just that the strategy was proven "effective" by a researcher. As one veteran commodities trader put it when asked how markets are created: "Ambiguity is the enemy of markets."[22]

As we've seen, a donor who is giving for psychic benefit is concerned with questions like *Will the money be used to help people? Was it spent the way I wanted it to be spent? Was it used effectively or was it wasted?* These questions are all about the organization's accountability. On a very fundamental level, the donor wants to be reassured that he or she can feel good about giving the money to your organization. But in a social capital marketplace, a "value-driven" donor asks very different questions:

1. *What outcomes can your organization produce?* What are the outcomes you are hoping to influence or have a track record of achieving? In other words, to what end are you doing what you do? And how do those outcomes link to things that others care about or are willing to pay for? You may provide some evidence of your ability to produce these outcomes, either research or track record, but that is background information.

2. *How much change in that outcome can your organization create?* What is your contribution to that outcome? For example, if the outcome was increasing SNAP (Supplemental Nutrition Assistance Program) enrollment, how many people did you enroll? This may also involve demographic information (for example, who are you enrolling?) or cost data (what is the cost per person enrolled?).

In short, the purpose of measurement in the social capital market is to show not only that you are making "a difference" but also *what difference* you are making. To be sure, stakeholders in the social capital market are still rigorous and concerned about effectiveness. But the threshold for "proving" impact is not as high as in the accountability world: logic prevails in the absence of statistical evidence. For example, it doesn't really matter to a retailer whether the food bank in their area can prove that its programs were the *only* reason why more people are spending SNAP food stamps in their stores; it's enough to show that their efforts made a *substantial contribution* to the outcome of increasing SNAP enrollment in that area. Stakeholders in the social capital market have a direct, vested interest in creating certain outcomes. Accountability is built in: there is value only if results are produced. If so, it really doesn't matter *how* the results were produced: whether the organization conducted the program as it was originally designed; whether the organization spent all of their resources on computers, offices, or trips; or whether they were wholly or partially responsible for the outcome. The value is in the outcome, not the program design.

My goal in this chapter has been to help you understand the difference between being accountable and impact and to help you see why a traditional donor will primarily be concerned with *whether* you're making a difference, while a value-driven donor will want to know *how much* of a difference you made. To be sure, psychic benefit and social benefit are *both* valid reasons for investing in nonprofits. But nonprofits that want to tap into the vast resources of the social capital market will need to shift their focus from accountability to value. In the next chapter, you'll begin to see how measuring the right thing can help you do just that.

# Chapter 2

# MEASUREMENT

To be able to measure value in the social capital market, you'll need to learn three basic concepts: (1) the difference between evaluation and measurement, (2) the difference between outcomes and activities, and (3) the difference between good measures and bad measures.

## The Difference Between Evaluation and Measurement

Frequently, nonprofits conflate program evaluation with performance measurement. Although program evaluation does use performance measurement, it serves a very distinct purpose. Formal, or academic, program evaluation is designed to test a hypothesis or *prove* a theory of change. For example, if you wanted to prove that distance learning (education via the Web) can increase youth literacy results comparable to classroom learning, you could "test" that hypothesis using a formal program evaluation with a randomized control group. The program evaluation would tell you, to a statistical certainty, whether that particular set of students, at that particular time, under that particular set of conditions achieved certain results. This is useful for academic research and certainly provides some assurance to donors that a similar program is a "safe" bet. But this type of research wouldn't necessarily enable a stakeholder to determine what level of performance or value to expect from an investment in a similar program.

Here's how the U.S. Government Accounting Office defines a program evaluation: "A program evaluation is typically more in-depth examination of program performance and context allows for an overall assessment of whether the program works and identification of adjustments that may improve its results."[1]

Because program evaluations are conducted by third parties, they can be costly; and because evaluations often involve primary research and data collection over a number of years, their utility to practitioners can be limited. Evaluations can also be difficult to interpret because they are typically written or conducted according to academic research standards. Here is an excerpt from a formal evaluation of youth development:

> Plasticity, then, is instantiated from the regulation of the bidirectional exchanges between the individual and his or her multilevel context (which may be represented as individual ↔ context relations). When such individual ↔ context relations are mutually beneficial, that is, when there exists adaptive developmental regulations (Brandtstädter, 1998; Lerner, 2004), healthy, positive individual and societal development should occur.[2]

In other words, kids' behavior can change depending on their environment! It would probably take a Ph.D. just to figure that out.

Too often, we engage in measurement "overkill." Nonprofits (and funders) tend to gravitate toward program evaluation as the only available tool, when less sophisticated and costly tools may be sufficient. Program evaluations are often misused by nonprofits seeking to demonstrate accountability or value. Case in point: A colleague of mine was advising a government agency on measuring the effectiveness of a drug use prevention program. The agency and several of its media partners had been debating how best to measure the results of their work so that they could be in the strongest position to show that their intended strategy was effective. The program involved an advertising campaign and direct outreach to youth serving organizations, including having children create a giant sticky note with a picture of themselves and their coloring project. The agency was considering a randomized control trial study over five years to isolate and prove the effectiveness of its media outreach. The randomized control trial (program evaluation) was projected to cost from $400,000 to $600,000—to determine whether coloring the logo was absolutely the reason why these kids did or did not experiment with drugs. There's a term in law, *res ipsa loquitor*, which means "the thing speaks for itself." This is one of those cases. In the end, the agency opted for a simpler pre- and post-survey to ask the children directly whether their attitudes had changed.

Another pitfall with evaluation is that nonprofits end up reinventing the wheel over and over again, by "re-proving" theories of change that have already been evaluated dozens of times. Many of these evaluations are not testing a new theory of change or novel program design for academic purposes; they are simply documenting whether or not this one particular program worked. But many of the programs that nonprofits are implementing today are based on established theories of change or proven assumptions that need not be re-proven. We know, for example, that the presence of a positive adult role model is statistically proven to insulate a child from risky behaviors like smoking and drugs. So we don't need to re-prove this theory each time a new program instantiates it.

That said, program evaluation can be a powerful tool and a useful one, when appropriate. The key is to first be clear on the question that you're trying to answer with measurement. In *most* cases, nonprofits are not being asked to prove that their program is effective with academic certainty using a longitudinal randomized control trial; rather, most often funders just want to know that you are relying on a proven theory of change and that your program is contributing to positive outcomes. That's where performance measurement comes in.

Although most program evaluations are designed to answer the question "Does a program work?" on an absolute basis, performance measurement is intended to answer the question "How well is it working?" on a relative basis. In other words, although formal program evaluation is attempting to prove a theory of change, performance measurement is designed to measure relative *contribution* to an outcome.

According to the GAO, "Performance measurement focuses on whether a program has achieved its objectives, expressed as measurable performance standards. Program evaluations typically examine a broader range of information on program performance and its context than is feasible to monitor on an ongoing basis."[3]

Performance measurement is quantitative—a number, a percentage, a ratio, or a dollar amount. Some examples of performance measures are a high school's graduation rate, total dollars raised, percentage of people placed in jobs, and the number of times a particular phrase was mentioned in the press. Metrics are calibrations—they quantify the *contribution* of a person, department, or organization toward a particular goal or objective. There are relatively few of the conventions or formal standards for measurement that exist in the accounting profession. And there are also few common performance metrics in the nonprofit sector, although certain fields like education, health, and the environment are beginning to standardize on a set of frequently used metrics.

## The Difference Between Activities and Outcomes

One of the most common mistakes nonprofits make is measuring activities instead of outcomes. An activity is defined by Business-Dictionary.com as a "measurable amount of work performed to convert inputs into outputs."[4] For nonprofits, that usually means your program efforts: teaching, training, negotiating, feeding, researching, and so on. Outcomes, on the other hand, are the changes that result from those activities—be it changed awareness, behavior, condition, or status. Outcomes aren't just for *individuals*—there are *organizational* outcomes (such as increased revenues, improved reputation) and *systemic* outcomes (such as changed policies, better incentives, increased investment).

Outcomes are all around us, and we hear about them every day. Barack Obama sold the electorate on one outcome: "change." Moreover, then-candidate Obama often used outcomes language to bridge differences in society and across party lines. In his famed acceptance speech at the Democratic convention in Denver, he stated: "We may not agree on abortion, but surely we can agree on reducing the number of unwanted pregnancies in this country." Abortion is an activity; reducing the number of unwanted pregnancies is an outcome. Here are a few anecdotes that help to illustrate the difference between outcomes and activities:

- *Buy a Van*. I once did some work for a community
  foundation, advising their program staff on how to measure
  the impact of their grants. At one of our weekly grant review
  meetings, a program officer suggested that her latest grant was
  pretty straightforward and didn't require much discussion: a
  grantee had requested $25,000 to purchase a new van. "How
  hard could that be to measure?" she asked. "They either
  bought the van, or they didn't. It's a simple 'yes' or 'no.'" I
  asked what the van was for. Delivering stereo equipment?
  Transporting stolen goods? "No, no," the program officer
  protested, "the van transports the elderly from rural
  communities to hospitals in the city to receive preventive
  care." As the conversation unfolded, it became clear that the
  grant wasn't really about the van; the van was just an activity.
  The real outcome of the grant was to increase access to health
  care for the elderly. And if that was the case, might there be a
  more efficient way to achieve that outcome? For example, they

could buy train passes for $10 per person and serve 2,500 people instead of just 8 people at a time in a van!

- *Back of the Yards.* A few years back I was asked to help measure the impact of a small charter school in a not-so-nice part of town called the "Back of the Yards." I met with the teachers, the principal, and a number of parents. Then I spoke with the after-school sports director. I asked him what outcomes he produced for the kids. He said, "The after school program has been a huge success—about one-third of the kids participate in our softball teams. As a result, these kids stay off the streets and don't get involved in gangs and drugs." Sounded good to me. "So what's the problem?" I asked. The director offered: "Well, we don't have enough money to expand the program or reach more kids. The board doesn't want to spend more than $10,000 on sports." So I asked the board what outcomes they value. They responded: "Student achievement, graduation rates, and teacher effectiveness." And what about the outcome of keeping kids off the street and not getting involved in gangs and drugs? How much of your budget would you allocate to that outcome? "About 10 percent." I asked, "Just curious … what's your organization's annual budget?" "$2.5 million." So the board would spend $250,000 on the *outcome* of keeping kids off the streets and not getting involved in gangs and drugs, but only $10,000 on the *activity* of sports. Bottom line: People value outcomes, not activities.

Another way to think about this distinction is the difference between counting and measuring. I was once hired by a federal government agency to help measure the outcomes of foreign aid. At my first meeting, the team I met with told me, "We actually don't need any more measures—Congress already requires us to report on 356 different metrics!" Here are some examples of what the department had to measure:

Number of facilities provided security upgrades with USG assistance

Number of public awareness campaigns about smuggling completed

Number of consensus-building processes assisted by USG

Number of technologies under development

Liters of drinking water disinfected with USG-supported point-of-use treatment products

and my favorite:

Number of cases of child diarrhea treated in USG-assisted programs

There's a lot of counting going on, and not much measuring! These were primarily "compliance" metrics—required checklists and activities that needed to be monitored for purposes of reporting to Congressional oversight committees. This type of measurement is usually mandated and is more of an administrative exercise than a strategic measurement inquiry. Nonprofits often have many of the same administrative or compliance metrics to report to funders.

Nonprofits typically focus on measuring activities more than outcomes for several reasons. First, activities are easier to measure: they are finite, tangible, and countable (think: number of hits to a website). Outcomes are tougher—more abstract, longitudinal, and complex. Second, activities are more controllable. Nonprofits can directly influence whether an activity happens or not (for example, did you hire a development director, did you put on a conference, did you mail fliers to a thousand people). Outcomes are harder to control—there are many factors that influence whether or not an outcome happens (such as environmental, economic, and geographic variables), and more valuable outcomes usually happen over time, which is often beyond a nonprofit's limited sphere of intervention. Finally, there are few donors that reward nonprofits for measuring outcomes. As we discussed earlier, most donors are focused on accountability and compliance, for which different questions are asked.

## The Difference Between Good Measures and Bad Measures

Finally, not all measures are created equal. The best measures abide by three simple rules:

### Measures Should Be *Credible*

By *credible* I mean believable and accurate. One youth development organization I worked with claimed that they were having a huge impact and cited some statistics that seemed super-compelling. The nonprofit claimed, for example, that although 14 percent of all teen girls in their region become pregnant, 0 percent of girls who attended their program became pregnant! And also, that although 53 percent of students graduate high school in their region, a whopping 95.7 percent of youths who attended their program graduated! Was this program simply extraordinary? Not quite. The simple fact that none of the girls who attended this program wound up getting pregnant doesn't necessarily mean that *because of* the program they didn't get pregnant. It might have been the case that the type of girls who were motivated enough to participate in this program were the type of girls who were responsible, did well in school, and were less likely to get pregnant in the first place! A more *credible* metric would have been "the percentage of 'at-risk' girls who attend the program and don't get pregnant." Similarly, the abnormally high school graduation rate could simply be explained by the fact that most students who took part in the program were already on track for graduation. A better, *more credible* metric would be "the percentage of students with poor grades, or who have tried to drop out of high school, who attend the program and graduate."

In another instance, a local charity wanted to claim that they had reduced the city's unemployment rate. But the city had a population of millions of people, and the charity was providing job training and credit counseling to only a couple of hundred people, ten or twenty of whom were successful in obtaining jobs. A better measure would have been the percentage of people trained who are successfully placed in jobs. Here's the point: credibility depends on your ability to make a *substantial contribution* to the outcome. Always make sure that your measures pass the "straight face test" and are backed up with research, plausible assumptions, and valid data.

## Measures Should Be *Practical*

By *practical* I mean that the data for the measure is reasonably available and does not involve tremendous effort to excavate. For example, one faith-based organization I worked with in Chattanooga, Tennessee, was focused on spreading the gospel through workplace recruiting. The executive director wanted to measure how many people they reached and how many people "found Jesus." The former was simple; the latter, a bit less practical. I counseled the director to create some meaningful "proxy" or substitute measures such as how many people regularly attended Bible study, or what percentage of those recruited became recruiters themselves (because they had such conviction about the mission).

Sometimes measures are impractical not because they're so abstract but because they are difficult to procure. For example, the Cristo Rey Network of high schools wanted to measure their impact on college *persistence and completion*, not just college access. In other words, how many of the students who graduated from Cristo Rey high schools actually went on to *complete* college. Practically speaking, that could require Cristo Rey to track data on a single student for up to ten years! Instead, we developed proxy measures for Cristo Rey based on research that identified the outcomes that were most influential in determining whether a student would enter and complete college (these were college knowledge, rigorous core curriculum, and financial aid planning). Cristo Rey could measure these outcomes *while students were still in high school,* and use this data as a "predictive proxy" for the likelihood that students would complete college.

## Measures Should Be *Relevant*

By *relevant* I mean that the measures pass the "so what?" test and are useful in explaining whether or not the outcome was achieved. The classic example here is the Nature Conservancy, whose mission was to "preserve the diversity of plants and animals by protecting the habitats of rare species around the world."[5] According to John Sawhill, the Conservancy's former president and CEO, for most of the organization's history it "would simply add up the amount of annual charitable donations it received and the number of acres it was protecting."[6] These metrics were referred to as "bucks and acres." They were easy to track, self-explanatory, and demonstrated a track record of success. There was only one problem: bucks and acres didn't really measure the organization's progress against its ultimate outcome: preserving endangered species. In fact, according to one Harvard biologist, the extinction rate at the time was as high as it was during the great extinction that wiped out the dinosaurs 65 million years ago.[7] More specifically, the species were declining *even in the areas of wetland that the Conservancy was protecting!*[8] As it turned out, activities outside the preserve (pollution, real estate development, and so on) were affecting the protected habitat. So simply measuring the number of acres preserved had no relationship to whether the outcome (preserving the species) was taking place.

Now the Conservancy has developed new, *more relevant* success measures to monitor the health of biodiversity and the abatement of critical threats. The biodiversity health measure is derived from the overall viability of conservation targets at a conservation area, and the threat status measure is based on the magnitude of the critical threats.[9] I use a simple test to make sure metrics are relevant: if you explain the measure to someone and they still ask "so what?" it's probably not relevant. Bottom line: Measures should calibrate your *contribution* to the outcome, linking your strategies to the desired change you wish to bring about.

The key to measurement is to keep it simple. Doing so isn't easy—there's a lot of complexity you'll have to resist. The nonprofit sector is teeming with all kinds of abstruse measurement frameworks, methodologies, grids, models, analytics, scorecards, standards, toolkits, databases, and workbooks. In a world of accountability, these are overwhelming; in a world of value, these are irrelevant.

Even those approaches that seek to measure "value" are primarily focused on value in an accountability sense—in terms of a donor keeping track of his or her investment. Take, for example, a thoughtful study by the Bill and Melinda Gates Foundation that analyzes eight approaches to integrating cost in measuring or estimating social value creation.[10] Among the approaches reviewed are "Cost-Effectiveness Analysis," "Social Return on Investment," "Best Available Charitable Option," and "Expected Return." Because the donors who created these models are not the actual beneficiaries of the programs themselves, their concerns are focused more on measuring the "return" on the donor's investment than on evaluating the quality and extent of the outcomes produced.

The measurement required for the social capital market is fundamentally different. Value is based on the *utility of the outcomes produced*, because impact is being "purchased" by stakeholders who have a direct (not a theoretical) interest in the results. Therefore measurement is, by necessity, much more organic. As Part Two will explain, the social capital market has created a new set of stakeholders, many of whom stand to gain or lose *directly*, and oftentimes *economically*, based on whether certain outcomes are created. Measurement is so much easier when people know what they want and what they value! Think about a real estate investor in a community who wants to gentrify a neighborhood because he stands to gain in property value if the crack houses are gone, the homeless are helped off the streets, and the community is beautified with public art. He has a *vested* interest in these social outcomes. The investor doesn't need a convoluted equation or two-hundred-page analysis. He just needs to know whether certain outcomes were achieved and to what extent. The value is in the outcomes themselves.

This chapter has helped you understand three key concepts:

- Evaluation and measurement are *not* the same.

- An activity is *what* you do; an outcome is the *result* of what you do.

- Your measures need to be credible, practical, and relevant.

The next chapter will help you to operationalize some of the measurement basics in this section. A few simple constructs will help you to "bottle" your impact so that you can sell it in the social capital market.

# Chapter 3

## CREATING A PRODUCT CALLED IMPACT

To demonstrate value to stakeholders, you need to determine which outcomes your organization can produce and then be able to measure your contribution to those outcomes.

Your mission is the key to unlocking your outcomes. But most nonprofit mission statements are very abstract and hard to measure. Take a few examples:

- *Ronald McDonald House Charities*: "To create, find and support programs that directly improve the health and well being of children."[1]

- *Boys and Girls Clubs of America*: "To enable all young people, especially those who need us most, to reach their full potential as productive, caring, responsible citizens."[2]

- *Free the Children:* "Free children from poverty. Free children from exploitation. Free children from the idea that they are powerless to change the world."[3]

- *The Smithsonian Institution:* "an Establishment for the increase & diffusion of knowledge … "[4]

These missions are not easy to measure. But frankly, neither are the missions of large corporations. Here are a few, for comparison:

- *Toyota:* "To create a more prosperous society through automotive manufacturing."[5]

- *Google:* "To organize the world's information and make it universally accessible and useful."[6]

- *Microsoft:* "To help people and businesses throughout the world realize their full potential."[7]

In fact, some corporate missions are even *more* abstract and difficult to measure than nonprofit missions. But for some reason, corporations don't seem to have so much trouble figuring out what to measure. Why? Hint: It's actually *not* for the reason that most people offer—which is that profits are easy to measure. The fact is, companies measure much more than profits; moreover, simply making profits wouldn't fulfill many of the corporate missions just listed. Rather, companies know what to measure because *they know exactly who their stakeholders are* and what they want! Corporate stakeholders include shareholders, customers, employees, business partners, investment analysts, government, and also NGOs. Whether we are for-profit or nonprofit, stakeholders drive our measurement—they tell us what is important to them about our work, and from that we determine what to measure. The key to measurement for nonprofits is not coming up with a fancy methodology or a whiz-bang software contraption to calculate "social return on investment." No, the key to measuring mission for nonprofits is the same as it is for corporations: let your stakeholders define your success.

## Engage Your Stakeholders

We love talking about "stakeholders" in the nonprofit sector. Frequently, I see the term used to signify just about anyone associated directly or indirectly with a nonprofit organization: government, donors, the general public, the "poor," staff, the media, and so on. One of the challenges with such a loose definition, however, is that we end up with a fuzzy sense of who really matters for our success. I define a stakeholder as "any person or entity who has a *bona fide* expectation of results from your work." By *bona fide*, I mean legitimate: based on either a contractual, an ethical, or a fiduciary obligation. There are certainly secondary and tertiary stakeholders too, but for purposes of capturing your impact, it is best to focus on your primary stakeholders. These are the people who have the most direct stake in your success and who will help you interpret your mission and understand the outcomes that are most important for your organization.

Like corporations, nonprofits have numerous stakeholders. But nonprofit stakeholders are different from corporate stakeholders. The primary difference is that in the for-profit world, customers have economic power (they vote with their wallets) and therefore have a significant amount of influence over the success of the firm. In a nonprofit setting, most of those whom we think of as "consumers" of nonprofit services (that is, beneficiaries) have little if any economic power. Because beneficiaries cannot afford to pay for the services they receive, donors and funders step into their shoes, so to speak, and proxy their needs by choosing the programs and services that get funded. Because of this phenomenon, nonprofits often treat donors and funders like "customers," giving them a greater voice as stakeholders. Every organization is different, and each must weigh its stakeholder interests according to its own value system.

Although stakeholders differ by the type of nonprofit organization, these are the most common categories:

- Constituents or beneficiaries
- Board members
- Senior leadership
- Key partners
- Individual donors
- Institutional funders

Each nonprofit must identify its own primary stakeholders. The process of identifying your key stakeholders is called "stakeholder mapping." To define your stakeholders, you can review your organization's strategy documents and interview key organizational

leaders (such as the trustees, the executive director, the development director, or the program director). When you're constructing
your stakeholder map, here are the questions you'll want to be
asking yourself:

Who cares most if we succeed or fail?

Who has a vested interest in our success?

Who influences our strategy or agenda?

To whom must we report our results?

To illustrate this approach, let's look at a stakeholder map
that was developed by a well-known charity, Ronald McDonald
House Charities (RMHC). The mission of RMHC is to find and
support programs that increase access to health care. RMHC is an
independent 501(c)(3) charity, and although supported in part by
McDonald's Corporation, it has many other stakeholders. RMHC
created its stakeholder map by interviewing key officers and board
members, soliciting input from staff, and using a third party to
conduct the analysis to bring in an outside perspective. Figure 3.1
shows what they came up with.

Mapping stakeholders is only the first step; to really understand
what outcomes they value, you'll need to engage them. This
usually involves one-on-one (in person, if possible) interviews and
sometimes focus groups. The answers may be different depending
on who you're talking to, but you ultimately will be able to see
similarities across all of your stakeholders. I call the compilation of
outcomes across stakeholders "stakeholder aggregation." Here are
the types of questions you want to ask stakeholders to "tease out"
(identify) their expected outcomes:

- How would you define success for the work we do?

- What outcomes do you value most about our work?

- Do you think we were successful last year? If so, why? If
  not, why not?

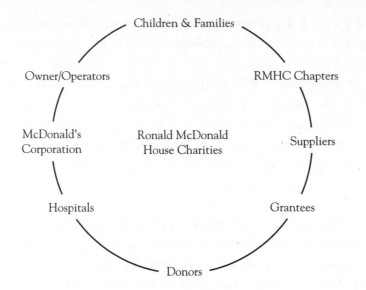

**Figure 3.1. Ronald McDonald House Charities Stakeholder Map**

- What's the ultimate impact that you value from our work? For example, in five years, how will the world look different if we are successful?

- What do you think the project needs to accomplish over the next one to three years to achieve this longer-term impact?

- What data or evidence would you need to see that would convince you that our work has been successful?

- What type of information do you need from us to demonstrate the value of our relationship?

- Is there anything we haven't discussed that you would like to add?

During these inquiries you will often encounter a lot of extraneous information. You'll need to sift through the information to harvest the nuggets of outcomes that will inform your work. Here are a few of the common challenges you may encounter in the process of talking to stakeholders:

- *Complaints*. Often when you gather stakeholders, they will use the opportunity to complain about your organization or about general issues related to the things your organization does. Listen respectfully, but gently shift the conversation to a discussion of what could improve. This will move you back into the areas of results.

- *Commentary*. Stakeholders, especially those deeply familiar with your organization, often begin commenting on your programs or specific activities. Shift the focus back to the *outcomes* they want from your organization. If they try to offer advice on how to improve your programs, ask them what improved results they desire from your work.

- *Definition of stakeholder*. Staff (and even the executive and some board members) may object to the notion that they are not considered stakeholders. Explain that those involved in producing the results have a stake in the organization, but it is different from that of outsiders. Your goal is to determine which people outside the organization will be the consumers of your impact.

Let's take a closer look at Ronald McDonald House Charities to see how stakeholders can inform your outcomes.

With 300 local chapters around the world, RMHC has become nearly ubiquitous when it comes to children's health. Their most famous program, the Ronald McDonald House, provides families with a free and convenient place to stay near a hospital while a child is receiving medical care. Other programs, like pediatric Care Mobile and Ronald McDonald Camp, are also designed to bolster the physical and emotional health of underserved children and their families. RMHC is a great example of an organization that's recognized the importance of stakeholder engagement—whether it's talking to the families they serve, the hospitals they partner with, or the McDonald's franchises that support them.

The largest RMHC chapter, located in Southern California, recently undertook an extensive stakeholder engagement project. "We talk about Ronald McDonald House as being a home away from home, and providing lodging. If that's really it, then frankly, it would be cheaper to have a hotel voucher program. We don't need to be investing twenty million dollars in facilities," explained Nicole Rubin, CEO of the Southern California chapter. "There must be more than that... We have all these anecdotes and moving stories about how we've affected families' lives, but that didn't capture what we know we're really about."

RMHC decided to refocus its efforts to measure their impact—focusing not just on the money saved by families forgoing hotels, but on all of the outcomes they provide to children, families, and hospitals. The organization wanted to prove that their compelling anecdotes were backed up by hard data.

So they turned to their stakeholders. RMHC of Southern California collected in-depth information from the families and the hospitals they served, holding focus groups with families in English and Spanish and interviewing hospital workers. They also formed an expert advisory panel including doctors, social workers, nurses, patients, a professor in hospitality management, and a corporate executive in charge of worldwide manufacturing and quality. The expert panel helped to synthesize all of the data that was being generated and to determine a framework that could be used in the future to assess impact on children, families, and the community at large.

Previously, Ronald McDonald Houses assessed impact by looking at the people served and occupancy rates. Although useful, these measurements were incomplete; for instance, occupancy rates measure the overnight usage of guest rooms, but no one was tracking how useful the House was to families during the day. During the stakeholder engagement process, the chapter gathered information from the families about services that they would like to see offered on-site at the Houses. Based on that feedback, the Southern California chapter will now be making more daytime and late afternoon services available to guests, including social workers, clinical psychologists, and child care (for the siblings of the hospital patients).

The chapter also discovered that although some important variables were already being tracked, other areas needed better measurement systems. They also implemented new guest satisfaction surveys as part of a national effort by RMHC to gather data from all of their houses and camps.

Another exciting part of the process was the chance to affirm what RMHC knows to be two key benefits of their program: *enabling family-centered care* and *creating durable support networks*. The first, family-centered care, is important because the family's active involvement in a child's medical care can actually help the child heal faster. Studies have shown that when a family can be active in the child's treatment plan and provide comfort to the child, it can reduce the length of a child's hospital stay.[8] Stakeholder feedback confirmed that both families and hospitals believe that Ronald McDonald House has had this effect. As Rubin says, "To see people attribute and credit Ronald McDonald House with that was really exciting. It's not just that we believe it, but the family and the hospital believe that to be the case."

The second major benefit is that RMHC programs allow families to interact with each other and create a durable support network during difficult times. RMHC has traditionally measured the financial benefits for families who stay in a House near the hospital, but now they are also emphasizing other outcomes that they provide to families, like these support networks. The Southern California chapter also measures a variety of other outcomes relating to the physical, emotional, and financial welfare of the child and family. For children, these outcomes include improved self-esteem and an easier transition back to "normal" activities after attending a Ronald McDonald camp. For families, one outcome is the increased ability to communicate with the child's medical team. "Our organization's mission isn't just to provide lodging," says Rubin. "It's really to help these families who have a child who's been diagnosed with something serious."

Stakeholder benefits extend beyond families. The Southern California chapter also measures and reports outcomes that are valuable to hospitals, as hospital partnerships are crucial to the program's success. In addition to the reduced length of stay due to family care, other outcomes valued by hospitals include improved patient satisfaction and improved outpatient treatment options for families who stay in a Ronald McDonald House. These are major benefits for the hospitals linked to a Ronald McDonald House.

Not only did these exercises in stakeholder engagement improve impact assessment, but the actual process of talking to stakeholders was also productive. It engaged the internal staff, the hospital partners, and the donors in thinking about what outcomes are most valued. "It shows a degree of seriousness about results that can distinguish one nonprofit from another," notes Rubin. For funders in particular, it has been very powerful to present results in a language that they can relate to. "The most sophisticated funders are very strategic these days. They want to know what is the impact of your program, and what's the impact of the money they're going to invest in you. I feel so proud of the story that we're able to tell. I definitely see how it's helped us in our writing of grants, in our story to funders and donors. It's really gotten people passionate about what we do."

At the global level, the entire Ronald McDonald House Charities organization is also heavily invested in the stakeholder engagement process, working closely with partners ranging from the health care community to McDonald's franchises and other corporate donors. As Vice President of Programs Janet Burton asserts, it comes down to "knowing each one of your stakeholders and understanding the language they speak."

When speaking with business donors, for instance, RMHC often emphasizes the economic impact of their programs on families and communities, such as the expensive trips to the emergency room that have been prevented by providing dental care and health care through the Care Mobile program. An audience of donors also tends to personally relate to metrics like the amount of time that a family was able to spend with a sick child because of the Ronald McDonald House. For a grant proposal, funders will be less interested in the individual anecdotes, focusing more on the aggregate data that shows the broader impact of the programs on communities and the health care system itself. For hospital partners, one of the most compelling measurements that the charity shares is the correlation between the children's hospitals ranked highest in the world and the presence of Ronald McDonald programs. Burton notes, "Being able to demonstrate a connection is a significant part of the dialogue when talking to a new hospital or one where the house is expanding. People want to be in the company of the best."

RMHC also has a unique relationship with the McDonald's Corporation, which has been supporting the charity since its inception thirty-five years ago. The relationship includes not only cash contributions but a complex web of collaboration and in-kind donations from McDonald's franchises and suppliers. For example, the Operator's National Advertising Fund (OPNAD), an association of franchise operators that collectively purchases advertising time, has funded television advertisements for the charity during high-profile events like the Super Bowl and the Grammies. The charity would not otherwise spend donor dollars on such high-priced advertising, but it is able to gain tremendous publicity from those ads. At the local level, RMHC works to keep McDonald's franchises and co-ops engaged and excited about the charity's work, making sure that the same sort of cultivation occurs with them as with other donors. Franchise owners and operators are represented on local boards and receive reports on key accomplishments and challenges, on organizational finances as well as personal anecdotes.

As you can see from this case example, the involvement of stakeholders in determining just what to measure—that is, what's important—makes a huge difference in your organization's eventual *appeal* to those same stakeholders. After all, if they've told you what they like, and you have set up the measurements to show that you produce what they like, you are two-thirds of the way home. That level of commitment is powerful in the extreme.

At the end of the day, measurement is really just about telling your story—the good things that happened as a result of your work. Don't waste a lot of time describing your activities and explaining what you do; "We have a house where families can stay during hospitalization" is probably enough. Instead, focus on the story of your impact: "Our programs help kids heal faster and help families develop networks so they can continue their child's healthy path. And to top it off, doctors and hospital administrators find that they can deliver care more efficiently as a result. The way we work saves lives, saves time, and saves money."

There are several unintended but welcome consequences of stakeholder engagement. You will deepen your relationships with stakeholders. Simultaneously, you will raise the visibility of your organization. You send a message that you care about their opinions and that you will act on what you learn. Most importantly, you demonstrate your strong focus on producing results that are valued by the community. In essence, the work you do contacting stakeholders is a kind of pre-marketing for anything you may do in the future. Many times these stakeholders have never heard from the organization whose results they value, let alone been asked, "How can I create more value for you?" When you do this work, you put the message out there that you are proactive, responsive, and responsible and want to succeed at the outcomes your stakeholders value.

## Define Your Outcomes

Outcomes are the building blocks for value in the social capital market. They are the predicates to your mission: the changes in attitude, behavior, condition, or status required to achieve your ultimate impact. Outcomes can be for individuals, for institutions, or for communities. By engaging stakeholders, you can better identify the outcomes that people value most from your work.

It is particularly important here to avoid confusing outcomes with activities. The explanations in Chapter Two, Measurement, can help you distinguish between these two concepts. It is also important to prioritize your outcomes. You can do this in two ways. First, you must prioritize the outcomes from among your various constituents and stakeholders (be aware that they may compete or overlap). One way to do this is to identify the outcomes that have the most commonality or "buy-in" from all stakeholders. Another is to rank outcomes from certain stakeholders higher than others, and use that ranking to "weight" some outcomes more heavily.

The second way you must prioritize outcomes is to focus on those that are within your grasp. Outcomes come in many different shapes and sizes. Some outcomes, such as raising the visibility of an issue among certain key influencers, are more near-term. Others, such as passing legislation, could take years. The chart in Figure 3.2—which I call "Penumbras of Impact"—can help you discern the outcomes that are within your sphere of influence. The rule of thumb is that these outcomes should be *proximate* to your intervention, or program, and achievable within the next one to two years.

When you draft outcomes, you should always start with an active verb (such as *maximize, grow, leverage, improve, reduce*), because outcomes represent a *change* that is taking place over time.

The RMHC Southern California Chapter used these tools to refine the stakeholder feedback and identify the following outcomes:

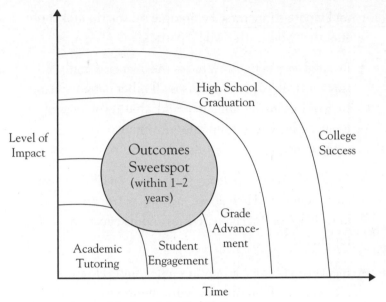

Source: Based on work by Ricardo Millett, Ph.D.

**Figure 3.2. Penumbras of Impact**

- *Improved treatment outcomes for patients:* What is the
  average length of stay for patients now? How can we
  connect RMHC activities to change in length of
  stay?

- *Improved support networks by connecting families of
  patients:* In what ways are families at RMHC
  connecting now, formally or informally? What benefits
  do they report from those connections? How might we
  improve those connections?

- *Improved patient satisfaction:* How does patient
  satisfaction at RMHC compare to a similar group who
  did not stay at RMHC? What changes at RMHC
  connect to increases or decreases in patient
  satisfaction?

- *Improved medical staff morale:* How can we measure and
  show the relationship between the work at RMHC

and reports of increased employee satisfaction for those
staff that work with RMHC participants?

- *Reduced length of stay:* What is the average length of
  stay for RMHC patients versus all other patients being
  treated for similar ailments? And what is the related
  financial benefit to hospitals or insurance
  companies?

- *Increased positive reputation for the McDonald's company
  and restaurants:* How do we measure patrons'
  knowledge of RMHC activities and its effect on
  reputation?

- *Increased sales for McDonald's restaurants:* How does
  awareness of RMHC affect customer revisit intent?

Remember that in the social capital market, stakeholders attach
value to outcomes, not programs. So getting these right is crucial.
But defining your outcomes is just the first step: next you'll need to
develop meaningful measures that demonstrate your organization's
contribution to these outcomes. In other words, how much of this
outcome can you deliver? You can use the measurement principles
in the preceding chapter to answer these questions.

## The Success Equation

One of the biggest challenges in "packaging" impact for nonprofits
has been the presentation. First, there is a big difference between
how you collect data and how you present it. Too often, nonprofits
present data to stakeholders in the same format in which they
collect it: spreadsheets; long, expository evaluation reports; and
complex charts or graphs. Second, when it comes to selling in the
social capital market, what is most valuable is the presentation of
the outcomes you *aspire* to produce and the level of contribution

you can make to those outcomes. The detailed information about your track record is supporting detail that you will provide to back up your claims.

Let's think about how one would approach buying a new washing machine. You would first want to know the outcomes it can deliver: *faster drying times, less wrinkled clothes, better stain removal,* and *lower noise levels.* Then you would want to check the manufacturer's claims, customer reviews, or *Consumer Reports* to evaluate whether in fact these outcomes are accurate. (This is where the difference between accountability and value becomes clear: stakeholders are *sold* on value; their doubts are removed with accountability.)

To sell outcomes, you'll need a simple presentation format that will help you lead with value and clearly articulate the outcomes you can produce and the way in which you measure your contribution to those outcomes. This is where a *Success Equation* comes in. A Success Equation is a simple tool that I have developed for nonprofits to communicate their impact. A Success Equation is not only valuable for communicating what you do—it's also a valuable tool to help your organization *organize* your thinking and work in relation to outcomes. In particular, the Success Equation answers the following questions:

- What are you ultimately trying to accomplish?

- What changes in behavior, condition, or status are required to achieve that ultimate impact?

- How will you measure your progress against those outcomes?

- What strategies will you use to contribute to those outcomes (and drive performance)?

The Success Equation is based on a few key principles. First, *parsimony.* Notably, it includes only three outcomes. Although some organizations may produce a veritable alphabet of outcomes, the Success Equation focuses on the *three most important* outcomes that your organization produces. By most important, I mean most influential over your ultimate impact. If you recall the concept of "regression" from statistics class, the "A," "B," and "C" outcomes are the independent variables, and the "D" impact is the dependent variable. If done correctly, when either "A," "B," or "C" is taken away, your likelihood of success with "D" goes down substantially.

The second principle is *outcome-centricity*. Too often, nonprofits think first about their strategies or programs and then try to measure what they get (that is, what outcomes transpire as a result of implementing x, y, z programs). This is a backward way of producing value. Remember, we're not just trying to "account for" or measure what we're already doing; rather, we are selling to stakeholders the value, or outcomes, we can produce (and then we are explaining how, through our program strategies, we will do this). So the Success Equation starts with the outcomes, listed at the top, and places strategies below them, to explain what "levers" the organization will pull to produce those outcomes. The metrics lie in between, because they calibrate the contribution of those strategies to the desired outcomes.

The Success Equation is agnostic to any particular measurement methodology. It's an organizing construct—a way of packaging and presenting your impact. The Success Equation allows your organization's entire mission to be summed up on one page, in a clear and concise way. And it allows any stakeholder to easily locate the key outcomes that your organization can produce. When we talk about "packaging" impact, this is one simple and compelling way to do that.

Figure 3.3 shows what a blank Success Equation looks like; Figure 3.4 presents a sample filled-in Success Equation.

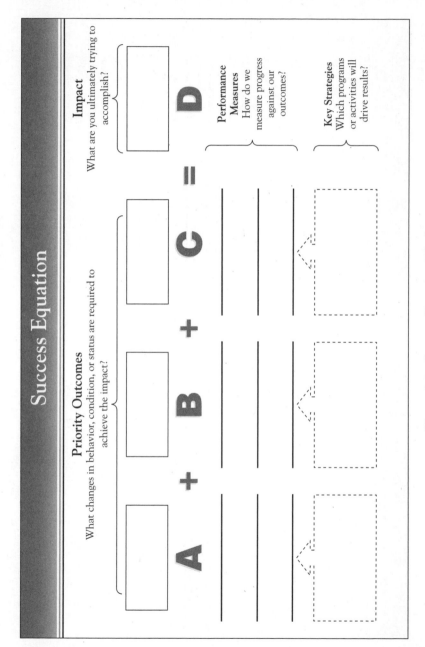

**Figure 3.3. Success Equation Blank**

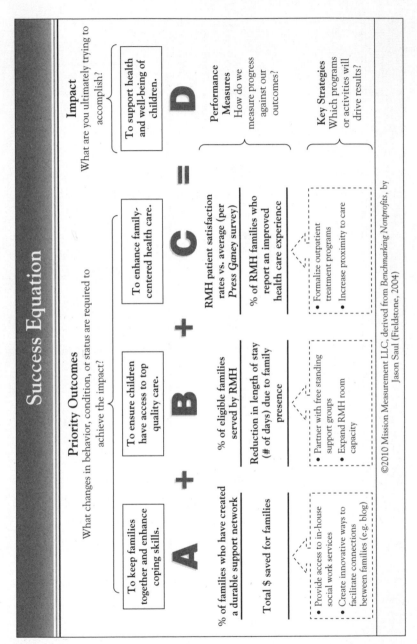

Figure 3.4. Success Equation Filled Out

## Boys & Girls Club of Greater Baton Rouge

To understand the value of the Success Equation in practice, just ask Keila Stovall, executive vice president of the Boys & Girls Club of Greater Baton Rouge.[9] "We used to say that we were an afterschool or summer program, and it was a big 'Aha!' moment for us when we started using the Success Equation," she explains. Their newly formulated equation lays out the organization's three priority outcomes: Increase Academic Success, Improve Character and Citizenship, and Increase Healthy Lifestyles. Each outcome is tied to specific programs at the Boys & Girls Club and can be measured by concrete metrics like grade promotion, community service hours, and pregnancy rates. "It has totally transformed the way that we communicate to those that are funding us," says Stovall. "Now they know that all the activities we do are very intentional."

The most compelling metric that the Boys & Girls Club produces is an impressive pass rate on the LEAP test, Louisiana's statewide exam required of every fourth- and eighth-grader for advancement. Given that most children served by the organization are on free or reduced lunches and attend low-performing schools, their achievements on the test have been truly amazing—and the key variable was their enrollment in Boys & Girls Club programs. Because the LEAP test and the flawed school system are such visible issues in the community, the pass rates produced by the Boys & Girls program never fail to impress. "There's nothing that has the same impact because there's nothing that's in the paper like our failing schools," says Stovall. "Nothing resonates quite like the academic success, because our public school system is in crisis."

The Club boasts impressive outcomes in its other areas as well. With childhood obesity a growing problem in Louisiana, the Club's encouragement of healthy lifestyles is another compelling data point, as charted by metrics like performance on the Presidential Fitness Test or hours of physical activity. Other programs, like the Youth Legislature or service learning activities, are measured by behavioral improvements and positive character traits. All of these results are showcased by the Success Equation. "We always measured outcomes, and we were always very proud of the outcomes," says Stovall. But the equation "made talking about what we do easier." The vice president is confident that it's the Success Equation that has allowed the organization to successfully pursue foundation grants and private donations. "For a brand-new project, starting a brand-new Boys & Girls Club, we were able to secure total start-up funding because of this," she asserts, adding, "I would be scared to think of where we'd be in this economy if we hadn't organized ourselves around this idea of communicating outcomes."

The Success Equation helps you to capture your impact in a way that is practical, measurable, credible, and meaningful to your stakeholders. Capturing your impact is a critical first step on the journey to selling your impact in the social capital market.

Part One has helped you to gain a better sense of the difference between the social capital market and the old "independent sector." In the process, you've learned about the difference between accountability and impact, the role of measurement, and how to define your "product" in terms of its most important benefit—its impact. Understanding these three elements will help you market more effectively to the social capital market (even as you continue to accept grants and donations from "feel good" donors).

Now that you've determined your key outcomes, the next step is to connect those outcomes to the market that values them. In Part Two, you'll learn about Marketing Your Impact.

# Part II

# MARKETING YOUR IMPACT

## How to Connect Your Value to the Market

### Key Takeaways

- How to create real leverage

- Discovering a new set of stakeholders

- The three highest-value outcomes

- How to improve your value

L everage is one of the most misunderstood concepts in the nonprofit sector. Too often, we think of leverage as a way to raise more money—*how do we leverage the funding we have received?* Yet there's another kind of leverage—the leverage that we use to influence others *in order to get the funding in the first place!* This kind of leverage is defined as "positional advantage" or "power." But I like this definition from the *Oxford Pocket Dictionary of Current English*: "the power to influence a person or situation to achieve a particular outcome."[1] For nonprofits, this type of leverage is gained by producing outcomes that people highly value and are willing to pay for. That's the holy grail in fundraising.

Frequently, I hear nonprofits bemoan their lack of power over donors—jokingly referring to themselves as "supplicants" begging for a handout or contribution. This is reinforced by the way we approach fundraising. Think about the language fundraisers typically use: *Prospecting. Cultivation. Development. Solicitation. The ask. A gift. Benefactor.* These terms imply a voluntary, zero-sum, unilateral relationship between donor and recipient. Complicating matters further, nonprofits are actually prohibited by law from delivering anything of value to donors! Hence the reason why most donor pledges are legally unenforceable: for any contract to be enforceable, each party must provide consideration—something of value. The law puts an even finer point on this: "[M]utual consent to give and accept is not a gift, but is an imperfect contract void for want of consideration."[2] And consideration "must have a value that can be objectively determined. A promise, for example, to make a gift or a promise of love or affection is not enforceable because of the subjective nature of the promise."[3] The bottom line: the typical way we approach fundraising—soliciting "gifts" from donors—is by definition inimical to leverage because we cannot offer anything of value in return.

The inability to offer value beyond the "warm glow" of psychic benefits has led most nonprofits to put their marketing emphasis on feel-good stories and pictures that elicit emotion. We are, quite literally, trafficking in the currency of psychic benefit. Yet that currency is becoming increasingly less valuable in a world of "psychic parity" in which there are so many organizations "doing good" (1.2 million in the United States alone). Between 2008 and 2009, there were more than fifty thousand new nonprofits created![4] And with only 1,100 different *types* of nonprofit programs (such as youth job training, homeless shelter, literacy, arts education),[5] there are, on average, over a thousand nonprofits for each type of problem! For example, there are over seven hundred breast cancer research organizations in the U.S. alone. With so much "good" to go around, selling *good* is becoming a commodity business.

All of this comes at a price: the way we are currently "marketing" our organizations to donors is both costly and unpredictable. On

**Table II.1. Benchmark Costs for Solicitation Activities**

| Solicitation Activity | Reasonable Cost Guidelines |
|---|---|
| Direct mail (acquisition) | $1.25 to $1.50 per $1.00 raised |
| Direct mail (renewal) | $0.20 to $0.25 per $1.00 raised |
| Membership associations | $0.20 to $0.30 per $1.00 raised |
| Activities, benefits, and special events | $0.50 per $1.00 raised |
| Donor clubs and support group organizations | $0.20 to $0.30 per $1.00 raised |
| Volunteer-led personal solicitation | $0.10 to $0.20 per $1.00 raised |
| Corporations | $0.20 per $1.00 raised |
| Foundations | $0.20 per $1.00 raised |
| Special Projects | $0.10 to $0.20 per $1.00 raised |
| Capital Campaigns | $0.10 to $0.20 per $1.00 raised |
| Planned giving | $0.20 to $0.30 per $1.00 raised |

*Source:* Greenfield, J. M. "Accountability and Budgeting, Assessing Costs, Results, and Outcomes." In H. Rosso, *Achieving Excellence in Fund Raising* (New York: Wiley, 2003). Originally published by J. M. Greenfield (ed.), *Fundraising Cost Effectiveness: A Self Assessment Workbook*, 1996, p. 281 (as cited in Wealth Engine ROI paper).

average it costs nonprofits $20 to raise $100 and as much as $125 to raise $100! (See Table II.1 for some benchmark costs.) Compare this to companies, which spend between $2 and $4 for every $100 of capital they raise.[6] For further perspective, the Obama presidential campaign spent an average of $4 per $100 raised (raising $750 million based on $30 million of fundraising expenses), while the McCain presidential campaign spent an average of $5 per $100 raised (raising $370 million based on $17 million of fundraising expenses).[7]

Why is nonprofit fundraising so expensive? Because we are spending a tremendous amount of time and money chasing donors over whom we have virtually no leverage and to whom we can offer little benefit. Even the state of the art in "donor prospecting" is still relatively crude. Most donor research analyzes a donor's *ability* to give (based on, for example, demographic profiles, wealth, and giving history) as well as a donor's *affinity* to give (for example, which types of causes they support). *Affinity* is where we find the weakest link. This analysis provides some bearing on who might be susceptible to an emotional appeal, but it doesn't really help determine who *values* or benefits from the organization's work. As a result, even the best nonprofits are engaged in a high-tech fishing expedition with pallid bait. As one national nonprofit CEO put it: "Who do we target? What do we tell them? Right now, we're fishing by throwing out a net. I want to be throwing a royal coachman to catch a rising trout."

Ours is a sector that is built on generosity, not leverage, and on appreciation, not value. As Katherine Fulton and Andrew Blau observe in their report "Looking Out for the Future":

- *Philanthropy is profoundly voluntary; by definition it is unforced.* Freedom and independence are proud features of what it means to be philanthropic, and any effort to dictate to others how they ought to give risks being rejected or simply ignored. Attempts to mandate or impose new structures and rules can constrain the creativity at the heart of much great philanthropy, or cause unintended consequences. Too many rules and requirements may simply cause some people to choose not to give.

- *Much of philanthropy is expressive rather than instrumental*—that is, the core attribute of much giving is that it expresses the values and beliefs of the institution or giver. As a consequence, an outsider's judgment that a gift is not "effective" matters less than the values it represents to the donor, the personal commitments it reflects, or the web of relationships it helps to maintain. As Harvard scholar Peter Frumkin observed to us, "At its core, [philanthropy] is about expressing values, not outcomes. Philanthropy is a vehicle of speech."[8]

- At the individual level at least, *philanthropy is often motivated by the pleasure associated with giving* (whether that pleasure is motivated by a true desire to serve or by the personal gratification that often comes with it). To make it more "professional" or "effective" is often going to make it harder. This is the paradox of efforts to professionalize philanthropy: complexity, assessment, and evaluation require expertise and diligence, but more professionalization creates the danger of losing connection to the very personal reasons why people give. That's why professionals, used to being strategic in other domains, often behave in very different ways when it comes to their private philanthropy.[9]

To create *real* leverage, then, we must think beyond marketing based on *affinity* to a world where we can market based on *value creation*. We need to think about shifting our focus from a self-perpetuating rationale (we exist; who can support us?) to a market-driven rationale (we create outcomes that others value and are willing to pay for). The greater the value you can create, the more leverage you will have. But how do we create leverage with donors who are looking for nothing in return? How do we change donor expectations? And how do we measure psychic benefits?

## A Value-Creation Mind-Set

Alas, we may be asking the wrong questions. The path to greater leverage with donors may not be to change donor behavior or expectations; the critical path may in fact be to *change donors*. The social capital market offers a new set of opportunities for nonprofits to appeal to a *very different set of stakeholders*. But how? By identifying the stakeholders with a *vested* interest in the social outcomes that you produce. The BusinessDictionary.com definition of "value" from a marketing perspective is quite instructive: "Extent to which a good or service is perceived by its customer to meet his or her needs or wants, measured by customer's willingness to pay for it. It commonly depends more on the customer's perception of the worth of the product than on its intrinsic value."[10]

In the social capital market, people "value" and are willing to pay for social outcomes that either (1) produce a direct economic benefit for them, (2) are necessary predicates to achieving an economic advantage, or (3) produce a desirable social change to which someone attaches financial value. Let's make these a bit less abstract by looking at some examples.

The most obvious form of "value" is a direct economic benefit. Although 501(c)(3) organizations are not permitted to take actions that "inure to the benefit of a private individual" as the IRS puts it, that does not mean that the *social outcomes that nonprofits create* cannot inure to the economic benefit of an individual or entity. In fact, economic incentives have been directly linked to charitable donations since 1954, when Section 501(c)(3) of the IRS Code was enacted, allowing donors to receive a tax exemption for charitable donations. In the 1970s, economists began studying the tax deduction for charitable giving, and they found that it clearly affected how much people gave. When tax rates were higher—and deductions were thus more valuable—people gave more.[11] Clearly there is a direct economic value associated with charitable giving.

Over time, social change has been linked to other direct economic benefits beyond the tax deduction. For example, a report released by the U.S. Census Bureau (ironically titled *The Big Payoff: Educational Attainment and Synthetic Estimates of Work-Life Earnings*) revealed that those who graduate from high school (a positive social outcome) can expect, on average, to earn $1.2 million more than those who do not.[12] That's a pretty tangible economic benefit. Corporations reap direct economic benefits from supporting nonprofits (research has shown a direct correlation between corporate giving and brand value, visibility, employee retention, customer loyalty, and even future revenues).[13] This probably explains why corporate cause sponsorships are expected to hit $1.61 billion in revenues in 2010, according to IEG.[14]

The link between social change and economic value can also be more subtle. Social outcomes can create an economic *advantage* for stakeholders—by either removing barriers or creating more favorable conditions. Think about the value to governments of improving a neighborhood and increasing the property tax base, the value to consumers of lower energy costs, the value to businesses of training people with specialized skills, or the value to health insurers of healthier lifestyles among their customers. The entire modern "green" or sustainability movement is predicated on the concept of monetizing the value of resource conservation and climate change. For example, take Coca-Cola and water. Water is the largest ingredient in the company's product, and clearly the company's ability to prosper depends on how well it manages this resource. According to the Global Environmental Management Initiative, "Coca-Cola is finding that source water protection is an effective business continuity strategy that can reduce costs, improve ecosystem health, and benefit the communities where it operates."[15] For example, since 1995, a Coca-Cola bottling plant in Brazil has invested more than $2 million in partnership with the municipality and other businesses to protect the Jundiaí River watershed, the primary source of water for that community.[16] As a result, two key sanitation projects (a new solid waste landfill and a new wastewater treatment plant) were built, dramatically improving the quality of the water reaching the reservoir.[17] The plant, which is the largest in the Coca-Cola system, also improved water use efficiency by lowering its usage ratio from 2.9 to 1.7 liters of water per liter of beverage.[18] This is a clear example of linking social outcomes with economic value.

Finally, value is created by producing outcomes that have significant financial backing. The laws of supply and demand operate in the social capital market too. Some social outcomes are more highly valued than others, and have greater "premium" associated with their achievement. Governments and large social investors allocate billions of dollars for certain social priorities, and fewer resources for other outcomes. This creates a certain "demand" for social change that is discrete and valuable. For example, the 2009 Federal Stimulus set aside $5 billion to "purchase" discrete education outcomes: improving teacher quality and getting better teachers into high-poverty schools, raising academic standards and creating better tests, using data systems that can track individual student growth, and supporting struggling schools.[19] The trend is growing toward outcomes-based budgeting in federal and state government, and this will create even more discrete value-creation opportunities for nonprofits. Other large social investors have set aside significant funds for such varied outcomes as eradicating malaria ( the Bill and Melinda Gates Foundation), creating positive youth development (the Edna McConnell Clark Foundation), and efforts to fight climate change by identifying sources of renewable energy (Richard Branson). In 2009, Vinod Khosla, one of the most respected venture capitalists in Silicon Valley, launched a $1.1 billion "green" venture capital fund to invest in new ways to address climate change.[20] While there are many other social priorities, the "market," or political economy, has put a higher value on some outcomes than on others; one way for nonprofits to create value is to meet this demand and supply these outcomes.

A value-creation mind-set allows your organization to operate more efficiently, intentionally producing outcomes for those who value them and are willing to pay. That is not to say that organizations shouldn't continue to market the psychic benefits of their work to donors as well; they should. But nonprofits will find greater efficiency, more leverage, and, perhaps most important, access to a much larger "economic pie," when they focus on outcomes that create value in the social capital market.

Part Two has three chapters: Chapter Four explains how to identify the best "buyers" for your impact; Chapter Five describes the highest value social outcomes, and Chapter Six teaches you how to increase your value to stakeholders.

# Chapter 4

## NEW MARKET STAKEHOLDERS

*Marketing is the activity, set of institutions, and processes for creating, communicating, delivering, and exchanging offerings that have value for customers, clients, partners, and society at large.*

—*American Marketing Association*

When we think of marketing for nonprofits we usually think of websites, brands, direct mail, and fundraising events—all are communications vehicles that help us tell our story. For traditional nonprofit psychic benefit donors, that makes sense, because our leverage with those customers is based on "story"—people getting excited, passionate, convinced, or otherwise emotionally connected to the descriptions of what we do. Think of the classic "Save the Children" infomercials with pictures of starving children that tugged on the heartstrings of so many donors. Story and emotion work fine for the typical psychic benefit donors. But the social capital market has opened the door to a new class of fundraising from a new class of stakeholders that I call "impact buyers." *Impact buyers* attach real value to key social outcomes and make rational decisions to "purchase impact." These stakeholders focus more on *value* than on *values*. So just who are these *impact buyers*, and how do you identify the right ones for your organization?

In the social capital market, there are five different types of *impact buyers*: service providers, upstream consumers, corporate partners, beneficiaries that can pay, and social investors (see Figure 4.1). Not every buyer will be interested in purchasing outcomes from your organization, but some will. These impact buyers are your customers, so it's worth knowing a bit more about who they are, what they're looking for, and how you can deliver value to them.

## Service Providers

Service providers value certain social outcomes that help them achieve their business objectives and enhance their service offerings. These may be for-profit or nonprofit organizations, but they are usually large enough that they can afford to invest in other organizations. These impact buyers include health care providers, educational institutions, financial services institutions, training organizations, social service agencies, and other intermediaries. Let's look at a few examples of how nonprofits can sell their impact to these stakeholders.

### IMD Guest House Foundation

IMD Guest House Foundation, located on the West Side of Chicago, is the largest urban medical district in the country. Home to four flagship hospitals with national reputations, the district receives 4 million patient visits annually and generates $3.3 billion in economic activity each year. The district is overseen by a commission that aims to ensure quality medical care, stimulate economic development in the area, and coordinate activities among the institutions. One of the Medical District Commission's initiatives was to open a guest house for patients and families. About ten years ago, the hospitals and the commission began discussions about launching a guest house and securing funding. At the time, the concept of a guest house was still evolving, and some medical

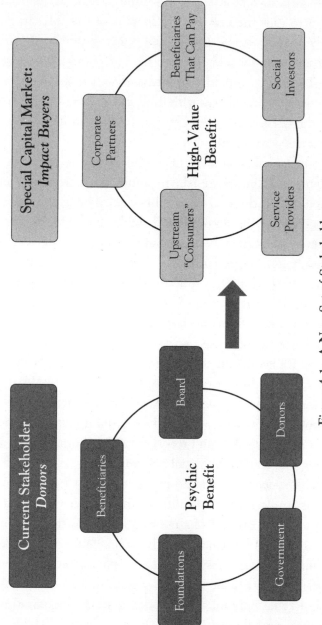

Figure 4.1. A New Set of Stakeholders

institutions and their leaders supported the idea more than others. The team working on the guest house quickly realized that it would be crucial to gain the unwavering support of the IMD hospitals, especially because many donors had existing relationships with those hospitals and would be more likely to fund a collaborative project. To secure hospital support, the guest house team would have to start sitting down with hospital leaders to prove that funding the guest house would be not only a charitable donation but also a wise investment.

As John Janicik, chairman of the board of directors, explains, the patients and families are "the most obvious benefactors" of the guest house, but there is also a business proposition here. "It was important for the hospitals to be able to provide this service in the increasingly competitive field of health care." A guest house can help a hospital attract a wider range of patients, which means that the hospital can build its reputation, garnering national prominence in certain medical specialties. An outpatient who drives into Chicago from another state for a test or a consultation could stay in the guest house, and a surgical patient from out of town could have his family stay there. Those patients might be choosing to come to Rush University Medical Center, for example, instead of heading to the Mayo Clinic in Minnesota or the Cleveland Clinic in Ohio. Guests are charged on a sliding scale, paying the full hotel rate if possible, and receiving a discounted rate or a free stay depending on their financial circumstances.

With the support of the hospitals, the guest house launched operations in a temporary facility in the district by renting and refurbishing ten apartments for use by guests. Courting the support of the institutions has paid off with a reliable funding model for the organization: each hospital agrees to pay a share of costs, and in return, the guest house makes a certain number of apartments available to that hospital. This model gives the organization the financial security of knowing that its lease expenses will be covered, and other fundraising can be used to cover administrative costs. The hospital, in turn, is provided with clean, furnished apartments, and the Patient Services group at the hospital has the discretion to decide which patients and families will use the facility.

The ultimate goal, however, is to move the guest house to a permanent, stand-alone facility with nicer amenities, so funding needs will continue to grow. This makes it increasingly important to remind the institutions of the business that the guest house is generating. Janicik explains, "It came upon us to call those who had stayed most recently at the institution, and ask, 'How important was it for you to have had a place to stay while you got your care?' Twenty-five percent said *that* was the difference." In other words, 25 percent of guests specifically chose to seek medical care in the Illinois Medical District because of the availability of the guest house. The institutions are now tracking this information independently, monitoring which of their patients and families are using the house and how the House is helping them to build their national and international reputations. The guest house has also provided the hospitals with information to help them understand the competitive health care marketplace—like how many guest rooms are available in other medical districts.

The guest house has been able to secure the necessary collaboration and funding by emphasizing their value-add to the hospitals and directly improving their ability to provide high-value services to patients. Janicik adds, "I'm confident that the hospitals continue to see the benefits of having a place for people to stay." For instance, after an unexpected event like a car crash sends people to the emergency room, hospitals can now offer a place to stay to families who would have otherwise been sleeping in the hallways. As these hospitals make their financial decisions, they are looking closely at the benefits that the guest house provides.

## Urban Gateways

This Chicago-area nonprofit focuses on bringing the arts to children in schools and underserved communities. Urban Gateways used to rely on federal funding through schools; however, much of that funding has dried up. But Urban Gateways found a new impact buyer: community and economic development organizations like the Local Initiative Support Corporation (LISC). LISC and its peers receive hundreds of millions of dollars from federal and philanthropic sources to revitalize underserved communities throughout the United States. The arts have become integral to LISC's mission: "Arts and culture increasingly are seen as key components of community development, just as important as housing, jobs and business to the life of a neighborhood."[1] For example, a LISC program called Building Communities through the Arts (BCA) is a multiyear demonstration program that incorporates the arts and cultural activities into neighborhood development strategies. Urban Gateways seized on these linkages to leverage new monies through anti-gang, recycling, environmental, and community revitalization efforts and to convert these fellow "service providers" into impact buyers.

## First Book

First Book is a nonprofit organization that improves literacy by giving children from low-income families their first new books. By providing new books to children in preschools and after-school programs, mentoring and tutoring programs, shelters and day care centers and beyond, First Book provides resources to empower teachers and administrators. With access to high-quality books, educational materials, and more, leaders can better teach, plan curriculum, and impart a love of learning, elevating the quality of the programs and opportunities available to children in need.[2] By purchasing millions of selected children's books from publishers on a nonreturnable basis, First Book had acquired significant buying power. The price per book, on average, is $1.80, including shipping and handling, and generates a margin of $.75 per book. Through market research, First Book realized that there were two to three hundred thousand programs serving children from low-income families; these organizations had an annual estimated book-buying power of $86 million.[3] To meet the demand of these fellow service providers, First Book launched the First Book Marketplace in 2004. As of 2007, more than twenty thousand service providers had signed up, and First Book's sales revenues were in the millions![4] The Marketplace is a perfect example of how an organization can create value for other service providers and leverage that value to generate significant funding.

## Upstream "Consumers"

Another set of stakeholders in the social capital market relies on social outcomes produced by others earlier in the value chain to achieve their desired outcomes and generate income. Just as there is in the commercial world, there is a supply chain in the social capital market. Upstream consumers can be nonprofit organizations, businesses, and governments. The following are a few examples.

### High School for the Arts

At a charity fundraiser recently, I was introduced to a young man named José who had just launched the first charter "public high school for the arts" in his city. José introduced me to some of the donors who funded the project: a well-known investment banker with a passion for the arts, directors from several different family foundations in the area, and a number of other arts patrons. I congratulated him and asked how it was going. He said, "It was tough raising the first $1.3 million, but we did it! Now all we have to do is come up with another $1.3 million next year, and the year after, and the year after ... " I remarked that that was a tough way to live. José said, "Yes, but there are all these rich donors who love the arts and they'll hopefully continue to give us money each year. Besides, what choice do we have?" So I asked José to share his organization's primary outcomes—not his mission statement, but the social change that his organization produced. Without missing a beat, he said, "We are developing the next generation of artistic talent in this country." I asked the young director who really *valued* that outcome the most. Well, I guess the nation's leading cultural institutions, because they're looking to recruit new talent ... and also the Juilliards of the world, because they want first dibs on most of our students ... and probably the music labels, talent agents, and Broadway producers. They are all harvesting talent from our school. Right. So I asked him, "Why aren't you *selling your impact* to those folks? These are your primary *consumers* of your impact—they *intrinsically* value your work (and stand to benefit from your outcomes)." I pointed out to José that this was his point of highest leverage in fundraising.

### Ronald McDonald House Charities (RMHC)

RMHC has been mentioned before, and it is similar in mission to the guest house discussed earlier. RMHC is useful to illustrate another point: to succeed, RMHC emphasizes another kind of value: helping upstream partners achieve *their* outcomes. In Part One, we discussed how RMHC had a variety of stakeholders: donors, McDonald's Corporation, franchisees, suppliers, families, and hospitals. From our research, one set of these stakeholders stood out in particular: hospitals. What we found was that children's hospitals *depend* on RMHC to make certain social outcomes possible—and these outcomes have a significant monetary impact for the hospitals. In fact, we found that 73 percent of children's hospitals in the United States have their own RMH or a Ronald McDonald Family Room.[5] When I spoke to the hospitals, I asked their executives how much they valued their local RMH, and their responses were adamant: "Of course! We love Ronald McDonald House! They do great work." That's a psychic benefit–type response. It was clear that the executives *appreciated* what RMHC was doing; but how much did they really *value* it? After all, some of these hospitals provided virtually no financial support to their local RMHs. "OK, I get that you like them," I replied, "but does it really matter to your business? What would change if the RMH didn't even exist?" When I got the hospitals to think like impact buyers, the responses were more revealing:

> You don't understand—RMH is critical to our business! There are many patients that *but for* the RMH, would never come to our hospitals; the families who stay at the RMH have much higher patient satisfaction scores, according to our Press Ganey surveys,[6] than non-RMH customers; RMH patients adhere to their treatment plans better because of their proximity to the hospitals; our own employees (doctors and nurses) have *much higher* satisfaction when they treat RMH patients; and finally, because of family-centered care and lower stress, RMH patients actually heal faster—allowing us to turn over more patient beds and significantly increase our revenues.

It became clear that these hospitals were in fact "upstream consumers."

## Corporate Partners

Typically nonprofits approach corporations through the back door, seeking grants from their foundation or sponsorships from their community affairs departments. Corporate funders have been stakeholders for nonprofits in the past, but primarily in the role of a psychic donor. Companies gave out grants because it was "the right thing to do" or because their CEO became emotionally connected to a cause. Local nonprofits could usually count on a corporation to buy a table or sponsor a benefit. But in the social capital market, corporations are becoming more value-driven, realizing that a growing number of social outcomes are directly tied to their business objectives: driving sales, growing market share, building deeper bonds with customers, and turning employees into brand ambassadors. This shift—from companies viewing nonprofits as charities to companies viewing nonprofits as business partners—has created the opportunity to approach corporations differently. Nonprofits can now walk through the front door to corporations, offering a business proposition about how particular social outcomes can create business advantages. Let's look at a few examples.

### Regional Food Bank and Wal-Mart

In one of my recent workshops, I was asked by the development officer at a large food bank who their "new" stakeholders could be. I turned the question around and asked them: "Who values your work most?" Their first response was "Well, probably hungry families—but they have no ability to pay for our services." With some prompting, the staffer continued: "and I guess local corporations, because if they donate food, poor people might remember their brand and buy it in the store one day … " I pointed out that donating food was really just a psychic benefit transaction; having worked with several major food companies, I knew there was no measurable business value to these donations—they were just the right thing to do.

But then I asked what the food bank's real outcomes were—was it just feeding hungry people or getting them to be self-sufficient? If the latter (which it was), I asked the fundraiser who she thought put the highest value on the outcome of getting families stable, and in particular, into the government-sponsored food stamp program (SNAP)? I asked her if she was aware that every \$5 in new SNAP benefits generates as much as \$9.20 in economic activity at local retailers.[7] And if you were to analyze where SNAP dollars in this country are spent, they probably favor the largest grocers. In 2009, the federal government will spend approximately \$50 billion on food stamp benefits at an average of \$124/month per recipient. Now imagine if the food bank were to go to the headquarters of

Wal-Mart (the nation's single largest grocery store operator), walk through the "front door" to their marketing department, and say "we're signing up one hundred thousand needy families in this state for SNAP—a big percentage of which will be spent at your store! That's over $12 million in new spending every month that we will generate through the social change we create: we want a $2M grant for this program now." It's going to be hard for Wal-Mart to say no. That's selling your impact to corporate partners.

### Youth Empowerment Organization

I recently advised a high-profile nonprofit organization whose mission is to empower young people to take action and help improve the lives of the poor in developing countries. Each year the organization engages more than 350,000 young people through its workshops and campaigns. When we spoke about corporate support, the development director pointed out that the organization has many corporate sponsors, the largest of which is a bank that pays a $300,000 annual sponsorship fee. She stated that the bank enjoyed the media visibility and felt it was a good cause to rally behind. (Again, a psychic donor.)

I asked the development director: "So what do you think it would take to get $1 million from the bank?" She said that the bank's sponsorship budget was pretty limited and the most the bank would ever pay for sponsorship was $150,000. Fair enough. But what if we were to shift gears and find a way to turn the bank into an impact buyer? Instead of asking the bank to sponsor our work in return for media visibility, what if we were to partner with the bank to generate direct business value? Banks make money on deposits, and banks get deposits by acquiring customers. The organization has access to 350,000 potential customers. Its mission is about engaging young people, having them raise money and take action to support international development. So what if they were to partner with the bank to create "social action" accounts that young people could open exclusively at this bank? The accounts could be used to save money for paying for volunteer trips or donations. And what if the bank, as a sweetener, could match the first $500 that young people put into those accounts? These "social action" accounts could not only further the organization's goal of engaging youth but also generate tremendous income for the bank. If only 10 percent of the 350,000 youth were to open accounts, and they maintained an average balance of $1,000, that would produce $35,000,000 worth of new deposits every year! Now how much would the bank value this outcome? Likely a lot more than $150,000. That's selling impact.

Here is one more example of how a nonprofit's everyday social outcomes can translate into business value for corporations when viewed through the lens of an impact buyer.

### Local Volunteer Corps

Not too long ago I ran into a friend who was on her way over to a local bank. She was raising money for a local volunteering organization that creates volunteer opportunities for local business executives. My friend was hoping to secure a $25,000 sponsorship for a fundraiser they were hosting. She figured that they would get good visibility and name recognition among all of the attendees. The way my friend was pitching the volunteer organization was a typical "psychic donor" appeal—"please support us, we're doing great work, and you'll feel really good if you do." I pointed out that the actual business value of sponsoring a benefit was quite limited and wouldn't carry much weight as a business rationale. Instead, I recommended that the organization approach the bank from a different vantage point: as an impact buyer. I had just completed some strategy work for that very bank, and I knew that they had developed a "top ten list" of top local businesses whose accounts they wanted to win. Because the program was based on recruiting executives from local businesses to do volunteering work together, why not offer to invite executives from the ten target businesses to volunteer *with* the bank executives? This way, the volunteer event still accomplished its purpose and also directly advanced a business goal for the bank! That's how you turn a psychic donation into a business proposition.

## Beneficiaries That Can Pay

In some cases, stakeholders directly benefit from your organization's work, and they are willing to pay for those benefits. Sometimes these benefits are financial, in the case of increasing a beneficiary's earnings or helping them to save money or access capital. Sometimes the benefits are nonfinancial, like health care, education, daycare, and other services of value. And sometimes the benefits can be indirect, as in researching a cure for a chronic disease that affects the stakeholder or supporting a school from which the beneficiary graduated. These impact buyers have also been called *repayers* because they are in effect "paying back" an organization for benefits already received.[8] According to one study, repayers represent the largest segment of donors: 23 percent of population, and 17 percent of donations.[9] The average repayer donated $11,000.[10] And when asked why they give, these beneficiaries answered, "I support organizations that have had an impact on me or a loved one," or "I give to my alma mater."[11]

Let's take a closer look at different types of beneficiaries that can pay, to determine how and why they do.

### Microfinance

Sometimes referred to as "financial services for the poor" or "barefoot banking,"[12] microfinance is the practice of making small loans to poor entrepreneurs, often in developing countries. It gained significant attention in the world of philanthropy when Muhammad Yunus won the 2006 Nobel Peace Prize for his work with Grameen Bank, which he founded in 1983 in Bangladesh. Microfinance is the perfect embodiment of the "beneficiaries that can pay" principle. Microloans—some as small as $15—can make a huge difference for people who would otherwise have no access to capital. Borrowers can pay rates as high as 30–40 percent, but they gladly consent because the loans enable them to improve their earnings and quality of life. As of 2006, there was $17 billion outstanding in microfinance loans.[13] One nonprofit, Kiva.org, boasts a new loan every thirty-one seconds and has facilitated more than $154 million in loans to poor entrepreneurs, at an average size of $385.[14] In fact, there are *so many* beneficiaries that are willing to pay (estimated at 150 million borrowers[15]) that microlending has become a huge business opportunity for for-profit companies. In 2010, SKS was the first microfinance company in India to take its stock public, raising $350 million in an IPO that was 13.8 times oversubscribed![16] Microfinance is aimed at the absolute poorest of the poor, many surviving on less than $1 a day. While this model may not work for all nonprofits, it certainly proves the point that even the poorest in the world can pay, if it makes a big enough impact on their lives.

## Kickstart

Kickstart is another variation on the theme of beneficiaries that can pay. This international nonprofit targets poor farmers in Africa and leverages technology to improve their economic self-sufficiency. Kickstart found a way to turn its beneficiaries into impact buyers by selling a low-cost manual pump (called the MoneyMaker) that helps farmers improve crop yields through better irrigation and, ultimately, generate more income. Kickstart makes such a compelling case to farmers that they take out loans to pay for the pumps themselves—costing sometimes as much as a quarter of a family's annual income. But it pays off: Kickstart increases net income to farmers by an average of 1,000 percent! In all, Kickstart has moved over 488,000 people out of poverty and increased their income and wages by close to $98.6 million!

Some beneficiaries are willing to pay for nonfinancial benefits. It just requires that the impact you create is significant enough that people are willing to pay for it.

## Joel G and Lymphoma

Consider my friend Jack, whose wife was diagnosed with lymphoma a few years back. Jack was a highly successful commodities trader, and he takes money very seriously. Still, Jack wanted to cut a six-figure check to the Lymphoma Research Foundation because he *valued the outcome* of researching a cure for this disease. I recall asking Jack, "Why them? If you found out that the Leukemia & Lymphoma Society had better results and was more likely to find a cure, would you give your donation to them instead?" Jack didn't hesitate: "In a heartbeat! I want to solve the problem. I want a cure for this disease." Jack personally values the work done by these organizations, and they have a direct impact on his quality of life. Jack is an impact buyer, because these organizations are producing a benefit that he values and is willing to pay for.

## Hyde Park Art Center: Not Just Another Pretty Face

The mission of the Hyde Park Art Center (HPAC) is to stimulate and sustain the visual arts in Chicago. It is the oldest alternative exhibition space in Chicago and boasts a long record of education outreach in the community. In the 1990s HPAC was looking for a way broaden the group of individuals that were patrons of the arts and facilitate a way for the artists affiliated with HPAC to display their work and connect with patrons. HPAC developed an effort called Not Just Another Pretty Face™. The participants ranged from highly established collectors to individuals who had never considered art collecting or patronizing an artist. HPAC mined its extensive list of artists (seven hundred in the Chicago area) to include a set of seventy artists that represented a broad range of artistic media and prices, career stages, approaches to the art-making process, and demographic diversity. HPAC meets with potential patrons to review and discuss the artists and their work. A member of the HPAC team follows up with each prospective patron to understand their interests and to develop a way to facilitate a match with an artist.

HPAC realized that there was an actual market for connecting new collectors to emerging artists. There was a demand from HPAC's beneficiaries, the artists, to expose their work and find new patrons. Artists earned thousands of dollars in new fees through this program and increased their visibility in high-profile collections. And the patrons experienced a direct benefit as well: they valued the opportunity to acquire new artwork at market value as well as the access to the art-making process itself that they wouldn't get when buying art through a gallery. In fact, both sets of beneficiaries valued these outcomes and were willing to pay for them—even the artists (50 percent of all commissions went to HPAC). There were a total of eighty-six commissions in 2008, and the Art Center netted over $100,000 in commissions alone. According to Kate Lorenz, HPAC's executive director, "We don't even use the term major gifts because this is so much more than that—we are building a broader group of people who are supporting art and artists."

## Social Investors

Social investors are people and institutions that place an explicit financial premium on achieving discrete social outcomes. This type of *impact consumer* differs significantly from general foundations or donors in two important ways: (1) social investors are outcomes driven and interested only in paying for results; and (2) social investors have allocated a discrete amount of funding to these outcomes. Nonprofits have greater leverage with these funders because their commitment to producing specific outcomes is explicit and professional, not gratuitous. Social investors can include government agencies, private foundations, high-net-worth individuals, financial institutions, and other intermediaries. Here are some examples of how social investors make decisions and allocate their resources.

# X PRIZE

The X PRIZE Foundation—made famous by the Ansari X PRIZE for the first to launch a spacecraft capable of carrying three people to one hundred kilometers above the earth's surface—is the consummate example of a social investor. This foundation has put an economic value ($10 million) on a discrete outcome, and it will award that money to the organization that produces the desired result. According to the foundation, "prizes result in rapid and widespread investment against a defined goal compared to the traditional philanthropic theories (i.e., research, pilot, demonstration, legislation, investment—a process that can take decades)."[17] There's no board schmoozing, no proposal crafting, and no historical track record required—it's just about the outcomes. In the words of the foundation, "An X PRIZE is a $10 million+ award given to the first team to achieve a specific goal, set by the X PRIZE Foundation, which has the potential to benefit humanity."[18] One of the current X PRIZEs is for the team that develops the first clean, production-capable vehicle that exceeds 100 MPG. Another is for the first team to send a robot to the moon. Future prizes in the offing include the following:

- *Energy:* A prize for the development of clean, renewable, cost-effective energy with minimal impact on the climate and the environment. Areas of investigation include alternative generation, energy efficiency, energy storage sustainable housing, and carbon sequestration.[19]

- *Poverty:* A prize for methods that "catalyze profit-generating firms to address major development challenges in agriculture, capital, education, health, and water." The goal is to highlight the most scalable enterprises that create wealth and uplift the widest set of stakeholders from poverty.[20]

- *Life Sciences:* A prize to focus on the "obstacles between cutting-edge scientific, technological and distributive understanding and the capture of those benefits by societies worldwide to improve health and ameliorate suffering."[21]

- *Exploration:* A prize to expand the use of space, the ocean, and other unexplored frontiers in order to improve life on Earth and extend life beyond the confines of land. Means would include "researching space and Earth's oceans; accessing and conserving their resources; catalyzing private, non-governmental activity; and tapping into our innate wonder about the Earth, the Universe and our place within each."[22]

The X PRIZE Foundation isn't the only organization to use prizes and competition as a way to accelerate social change. McKinsey estimates that the total funds available from large prizes has more than tripled over the last decade to surpass $375 million, and the total size of the prize sector could be as much as $1 to $2 billion.[23] According to McKinsey, "even-larger prizes may be on the way: several political leaders have recently proposed massive inducement prizes ranging from a $300 million award for the creation of high-performance car batteries to a staggering $80 billion pool of prize money to encourage the development of new drugs."[24]

Prizes are just one form of social investment. As the stakes for social change continue to increase, exciting new social investment vehicles are emerging on an almost constant basis.

### Social Impact Bonds

Created by Social Finance, a UK-based nonprofit organization, the "Social Impact Bond" is a perfect illustration of the way social investors are beginning to operate in the social capital market.

The innovative financial instrument is designed to generate pro-
ceeds from investors, which are then applied to schemes to solve
social problems. If they succeed, they will save the taxpayer large
amounts of money, a portion of which will be shared with the
bond's investors.[25]

Social Finance views Social Impact Bonds as a unique funding
mechanism that aligns the interests of key stakeholders around
social outcomes:

- *Government*—the public sector pays only for positive
  outcomes by releasing a proportion of savings to Social Impact
  Bond investors. Success payments are calculated such that, if
  Social Impact Bond-funded services improve outcomes, these
  payments will cover the costs of the interventions. This
  enables investors to make a return. Investors carry the risk
  that funded interventions may fail to improve outcomes.

- *Social investors*—investment in Social Impact Bonds by
  trusts and foundations, commercial investors, and high net
  worth individuals offers an opportunity to generate a blended
  social and financial return on investment. The social and
  financial imperatives are aligned; investors receive greater
  financial return as the social return improves.

- *Social service providers*—Social Impact Bond investment is
  used to pay upfront for the delivery of services. This enables
  providers of all sizes to participate in generating success.
  Providers are encouraged to innovate in order to achieve the
  best possible outcomes for the target population. The focus
  is on the social value that service providers can offer, rather
  than on the cost of services alone.[26]

The first such bond, called the "Re-Offending Social Impact
Bond," was introduced in March 2010 by the U.K. Ministry of

Justice. The bond will raise up to $7.5 million to finance various social sector organizations to work closely for six years with three thousand short-term prisoners jailed in the Peterborough Prison, both inside prison and after their release, to help them resettle into the community. If this initiative reduces reoffending by 7.5 percent or more, investors will receive from the Ministry a share of the long-term savings. At present, reoffenders cost the UK government a fortune: of the 40,200 adults on short-term sentences, an estimated 60 percent will go on to reoffend within a year of release, at a significant cost to the taxpayer and society.[27] If the bond delivers a drop in reoffending beyond the threshold, investors will receive an increasing return the greater the success at achieving the desired social outcome, up to a maximum of 13 percent.

According to the *Economist*:

> The social-impact bond would also shift the focus of contract negotiations toward the impact on society, rather than the less risky output-based measurements that are typical in existing outsourcing contracts. The current model of private finance for public services tends to focus chiefly on reducing the cost of the current activity (i.e., housing prisoners). Sometimes there are performance elements (e.g., penalties for letting prisoners escape), but what is new about the government's scheme is that it incorporates incentives for radically improving outcomes (i.e., helping them stay out of jail) into the financing model. The aim is to attract innovative social problem-solvers in both the for-profit and nonprofit sectors, although the pilot scheme only uses non-profits. The frustrations of the non-profit sector with the inadequate funding of preventive policies under the present system, and the prospect that the current economic mess will only make things worse, prompted the bond's creation.[28]

David Hutchison, chief executive of Social Finance, sees this as the future of social investing: "The Social Impact Bond has the potential to unlock an unprecedented flow of finance for social sector organizations. By focusing returns on outcomes, these organizations will be incentivized to develop innovative interventions to tackle ingrained social problems which weigh heavily on our society and our national purse."[29]

### The Robin Hood Foundation

Founded by Paul Tudor Jones, a successful hedge fund manager, the Robin Hood Foundation (RHF) aims to fight poverty in New York City. RHF raises money privately and funds organizations that demonstrate measurable results. The funding is 100 percent outcome-based. RHF is built on a complex system of metrics that calculates the success of a grant by estimating its benefit to the poor per dollar of cost to Robin Hood. RHF compares grants based on their "poverty-fighting effectiveness" and uses a common cost/benefit ratio to determine which grant will yield the greatest "return" for its philanthropic investment. According to RHF: "To estimate benefit-cost ratios for Robin Hood's grants, we monetize the value of the immediate outcomes. Health clinics diagnose and treat asthma. How much better off are patients who receive these interventions? Schools help at-risk students to graduate. How much does graduation boost future earnings? Micro-lending grants help women entrepreneurs set up home businesses. By how much can these women expect their future earnings to rise?"[30] In fact, RHF takes measuring success so seriously it wrote an entire hundred-page-plus manifesto just on that topic alone. In 2010, RHF raised a jaw-dropping $87.8 million in one night, 100 percent of which will go to organizations that generate measurable results. RHF is the epitome of a social investor who "values" discrete outcomes, and pays for results.

These are just a few snapshots of each category of impact buyer, how they operate and what they value. Now it's time to think about the impact buyers for your organization's outcomes.

## Finding the Fulcrum: Who Are Your Impact Buyers?

The first question any marketer will ask you is "Do you know who your customers are?" Nonprofits are not used to asking this question or even thinking about it. As we discussed in Part One, many nonprofits are torn between two sets of stakeholders: *beneficiaries* (those who "value" but usually cannot pay for programs or services) and *funders* (those who pay the freight for programs and services but do not receive any benefits from them). In the social capital market, there is a new set of stakeholders whom I refer to as *impact buyers*—those who are willing to pay for the outcomes you produce. Every nonprofit has impact buyers, regardless of mission or size.

The key to identifying your organization's impact buyers is to zero in on the people for whom you are creating the most value. Start with the outcomes you identified in the Success Equation exercise in Part One and consider the following leverage questions:

- Who puts the biggest premium on what you're doing?

- What is the economic value of your work?

- Who is willing to pay for your outcomes?

- Who is in pain because they're not getting what you produce?

- Who has a financial incentive to help you?

- If you ceased to exist, who would substitute for your work?

These are tough questions, ones that we don't often ask of ourselves. Yet they are critical to helping tease out the leverage points for your organization and identify the people or organizations that derive the greatest benefit from your work. To be an *impact buyer*, prospective donor will need to meet three criteria:

1. *Ability to pay*: Does the prospective impact buyer have significant financial resources?

2. *Clearly stated outcomes*: Are there clear social impacts that the prospective buyer has prioritized?

3. *High level of value associated with outcome or result*: Will the person or entity have less "pain," gain significant advantage, or realize an economic benefit if the social impact is achieved?

Even organizations that may seem purely altruistic—like arts institutions or animal rights groups—have impact buyers. Discovering them just requires some creativity and entrepreneurial thinking. Over the years, in workshops and in the classroom, nonprofit leaders have asked me, "Does this apply to my organization? How do we find our impact buyers?" Here are some of the vignettes from those conversations, which help illustrate how this framework can be applied to a range of different organizations and causes.

### "What About the Spotted Owl?"

Some social missions appear to be purely public goods that have no market value. Saving the spotted owl is a case in point. It seems to defy all of the leverage questions: although many appreciate the owl, there's a perception that no one will suffer financially if the species disappeared, and no one appears to have any economic interest in saving the owl. So how can there be any impact buyers for this outcome? The problem here is that we are framing the outcome too narrowly. Sure, it seems no one *really* values the spotted owl *per se*, but the owl is just one of many species that animal lovers care about. Although the owl may appear to have no obvious economic value, the people who love owls certainly do. Consider these facts: the Humane Society of the United States boasts over eleven million members and constituents, and animal lovers spent over $45 billion in 2009.[31] Now who cares about the spotted owl? I bet many corporations would. If you can't value the outcome, you can always value the people who value the outcome.

### "I Run an Arts Organization; Who Values That?"

The arts may appear to be another public good, but that, too, is not always the case. The Hyde Park Art Center, mentioned earlier, showed that there are beneficiaries who are willing to pay, provided you can offer compelling value. Operas, symphonies, and theatres have done the same—finding corporations and individuals who are more than willing to pay for the entertainment value received and thereby to subsidize the cost of educational and other programs for underserved communities. Urban Gateways showed how the arts can be used to create valuable outcomes for community and economic development.

### "My Constituents Are the Homeless, They Have No Ability to Pay."

Although the homeless may not be a highly desirable commercial demographic, the *absence* of the homeless is a desirable economic outcome. Large property owners, restaurants, and other local businesses all have an economic interest in gentrifying the community. Not to mention local government, which has a direct interest in increasing property values and therefore tax receipts. Local government also benefits through lower costs: a Colorado study found that providing supportive services to the homeless saved an average of $31,545 per individual, with total savings of $4.7 million to the state.[32] Local government, property owners, and local businesses are all *service providers* with a clear economic stake in achieving this outcome.

### "We're a Big Museum; Everyone Comes for Free."

A few years back we were asked by the Smithsonian to help measure the impact of the Museum of Natural History. One of the outcomes we identified was raising awareness among young people about their impact on the environment. For example, one exhibit illustrated the effects of antiperspirant manufacturing on aluminum deposits, and another showed what SUVs can do to our climate. In addition to being a world class research facility, the Museum is among the most trafficked in the world, with 7.5 million visitors a year.[33] Although those beneficiaries aren't likely to pay (the Smithsonian is free for all visitors), there are many *social investors* who would highly value the opportunity to influence that many young people, particularly as it relates to the environment.

*"Our Organization Helps Kids Who Are Juvenile Delinquents."*

Minnesota-based Boys Totem Town is a residential correctional facility for adolescent boys ages twelve through nineteen who have been adjudicated delinquent by the courts. While these boys may appear to have no immediate economic value, that's not to say that they could not be trained in specialized skills that would make them valuable. Now consider that Minnesota is home to the biggest bicycle parts supplier in North America and, presumably, the world; the largest bike tool manufacturer; two of the nation's leading bike retailers; the largest distributor of road biking goods and apparel; and one of the premier triathlon shops in the country.[34] All in all, the bike business in Minnesota accounts for approximately $315 million per year in revenues, on par with the size of forestry and fishing![35] It's unlikely that this thriving industry has an already well-developed pipeline of future talent—people who are trained in bike production, maintenance, service, and sales. But if Boys Totem Town developed one, it's likely that the bike industry could become upstream consumers of this specialized talent.

These examples are helpful in illustrating the dexterity and creative thinking that's required to uncover sometimes less obvious impact buyers. But there are some principles behind the magic—tips you can use to help tease out your organization's own *impact buyers*. Here are four strategies you can follow:

1. *Follow your outcomes upstream.* Sometimes it's not immediately apparent who would value your outcomes. But if you construct a mini value-chain, you can identify those upstream players who thrive off of the work that you are doing.

Start with your own outcomes: Who depends on those as inputs for the way they produce value? Take the anecdote I discussed earlier about the food bank and Wal-Mart. The initial "buyers" that the organization suggested (that is, "hungry families") didn't pass muster, but as we worked through the logic of who benefited from their outcomes, and we followed those benefits upstream, the true customers came into focus. It just took a bit of imagination and some simple research to determine that large retailers, and Wal-Mart in particular, benefited directly from the outcome of increased food stamp enrollment. The performing arts high school followed the same logic: we modeled the pathway of talented performers who graduated, and we identified their "consumers": the recording studios, colleges, and cultural institutions who had a self-interest in acquiring them.

2. *Revalue your existing stakeholders.* Sometimes your impact buyers are right in front of you; you may just be looking at them in the wrong light. Think about RMHC: they partnered closely with hospitals and were thankful for the donated land and occasional philanthropic support from the hospital foundations. But now that RMHC is in a position to demonstrate the economic value they create for hospitals, they can approach hospitals as impact buyers and generate significantly greater support. The same goes for another organization I advised that works with universities to engage students around social responsibility. The nonprofit receives donations from students and even corporations, but not from the schools themselves (many of which are elite MBA graduate programs). That's because most schools view the organization as a charity promoting ethics and social responsibility among students. But what was once "charitable" has now gained real economic import: universities are increasingly focusing on social responsibility curricula to

recruit top students and place them in top jobs (a survey of about one hundred MBA programs by the Aspen Institute, a Washington, D.C., think tank, found that the number of "social responsibility-related" courses offered by the schools jumped 60 percent between 2005 and 2009).[36] As universities are eager to improve their offerings on sustainability and social responsibility, this organization is in a position to create direct value for schools and convert them into impact buyers.

3. *Leverage your other assets.* Another way to identify potential impact buyers is to redeploy your capabilities or assets in new ways that create value for others. Ask yourself, *What competencies have we developed, what reach do we have, what problems did we solve that can be of value to others?* I recently toured Me to We, a Canadian social enterprise that designed its own eco-friendly line of clothing. The executive director described how the organization took great pains to piece together a supply chain that was 100 percent "sustainable," from organic cotton all the way to ethical production. I pointed out that there were many corporations struggling to build the same thing, and that Me to We's supply chain is an asset they could "sell" to other companies. First Book is another case in point: the organization realized that its core competency—buying millions of children's books each year at steep discounts—could be of value to peer organizations. By leveraging its market power and "selling" it to other youth-serving organizations, First Book is able to help them save millions of dollars and become impact buyers. The Humane Society of the United States has been able to turn corporations into impact buyers by using the buying power of its 11 million constituents to reward companies that pledge to avoid animal testing. And the Hyde Park Art Center realized that it had an unleveraged asset: emerging artists. By recognizing that patrons would pay to be able to commission

works from these artists, HPAC found that it could advance its mission and convert many of the museum's members and friends into impact buyers.

4. *Look for beneficiaries who can pay.* Although most people served by nonprofits are disadvantaged, not all are without means to pay for services, particularly if those services have a clear economic benefit. Community colleges, vocational schools, and universities are all financed largely by their own beneficiaries (the students), who value the return on investment. Many nonprofits are designing state-of-the-art job training to teach highly marketable skills like video game programming, web design, and video production: these programs could be offered with tiered pricing, so that those who could afford to pay could subsidize the offerings for others.

Impact buyers represent an entirely new market for nonprofits. In this chapter, you learned about five types of impact buyers: corporate partners, beneficiaries that can pay, social investors, service providers, and upstream consumers. To be successful with these buyers, nonprofits must focus on creating higher-value outcomes. It's not just about doing good work and hoping it adds up to something or counting results to prove that you are effective. Though psychic benefits are important, outcomes trump feelings in the social capital market. Buyers in the social capital market are looking for value—programs and services that produce outcomes that people are willing to pay for. The next chapter tells you how to refine your outcomes to increase their value to impact buyers.

# Chapter 5

# NOT ALL OUTCOMES ARE CREATED EQUAL

In recent years, consultants and fundraisers have encouraged nonprofits to be "outcomes-driven" and focus on results to increase their appeal to funders. That's certainly better than the opposite. But that's only half the story. It's not just about producing *an* outcome; it's about producing *high-value* outcomes. The fact is, not all outcomes are created equal. For example, giving winter coats to the homeless is a nice outcome, one that may appeal to psychic benefit donors. But helping an individual get off the streets and become financially self-sufficient is more valuable to stakeholders in the social capital market. It turns out there are different levels of outcomes—*degrees of impact*—some of which carry greater currency in the social capital market than others. This chapter describes the three highest-value outcomes and explains how they can be applied to any aspect of social change.

A few years ago I was advising a Fortune 500 company on measuring the impact of its philanthropy. The funder valued positive youth development outcomes; in particular, reducing risky behaviors like the use of alcohol, tobacco, and drugs. One year, the giving officer had to make a decision between two grant opportunities: one grant reached 240,000 kids, the other reached 30,000 kids. But when the company looked beneath the surface to analyze what "impact" it would be buying, the answer wasn't so clear. The organization reaching 240,000 kids was mailing flyers to 240,000 girls encouraging them to play golf. The organization serving 30,000 kids was matching youth with positive adult role models to develop "protective factors" that would inoculate youth against risky behaviors. Now guess which program the corporation funded. If it were just a matter of public relations, the company might have funded the bigger number of kids reached. But the corporation "valued" the outcome of changing youth behavior (because its business depended on it) and therefore invested in the organization that created the "higher value" outcome.

Procter & Gamble illustrates the same point differently. When the company first launched its Pampers campaign in partnership with UNICEF, they hired a PR firm to conduct focus groups with moms, their core constituents. P&G explained the partnership with UNICEF, and the fact that maternal and newborn tetanus is a preventable disease, responsible for the death of one baby approximately every three minutes and the loss of up to thirty thousand mothers each year. Then the company announced that for every package of Pampers they bought, P&G would donate seven cents to UNICEF. Moms were nonplussed. Seven cents? That's it? So P&G decided to go back to the drawing board and convened a new focus group of moms, this time presenting a different proposition: *For every pack of Pampers you buy, Pampers will provide UNICEF with funding for one life-saving tetanus vaccine that will benefit a woman in need and her newborn in one of seventeen developing countries. By buying a pack of Pampers, you will save a life.* The response was overwhelmingly positive. Here's the great part: The cost of one tetanus vaccine? Seven cents. In this case, consumers valued real impact, not just efforts. This further illustrates the point that not all levels of "doing good" are the same—the market values certain outcomes more than others.

When you look across all of the work that gets funded in the nonprofit sector—regardless of the type of program or issue—there are three outcomes that emerge as the most likely to win funding.

I share these below. But first, let me explain how I identified these. Over the past five years I have measured the outcomes of thousands of nonprofit organizations, and analyzed the impact of over $950 million of funding.[1] Through my work, I catalogued hundreds of different types of outcomes—eventually leading to the first framework of common outcomes for the nonprofit sector, which I developed together with the Urban Institute.[2] After we completed that project, I revisited the data. Over time, another "aha" emerged: when I analyzed the outcomes of the organizations that were most successful at attracting funding—and also the outcomes that funders said were the most important—it became clear that there were three types of outcomes that stood out, which I call "high-value outcomes."

- *Change in status or condition.* This is the ultimate impact for direct service organizations, but is also applicable to other nonprofit missions. As opposed to smaller, more incremental changes, what I call "fragments of an outcome" (such as providing meals to the hungry or giving coats to the homeless), changing the status is about creating a more durable social impact. There are many different ways to change someone's status: economic status (such as employment); social status (such as civil rights); physical status (for example, from disabled to self-sufficient); or intellectual status (such as literacy). A change in status can also apply to an organization, such as through capacity building to become financially sustainable or through compliance to become a "socially responsible" corporation.

- *Return on investment (ROI).* ROI in this context means making the case that your organization can produce social or economic value that far exceeds the cost. Nonprofits can demonstrate ROI by showing a direct correlation between inputs (the dollars invested in your nonprofit) and outputs or returns (the quantifiable benefits produced by your organization). For example, the Robin Hood Foundation measures a benefit-cost ratio that estimates the economic value created for every dollar spent—in 2007, that was 18:1 (meaning the average $1 granted by Robin Hood yields an estimated $18 in future revenue for a New Yorker in need[3]). Kickstart has a similar ROI calculation—something it calls the Bang for Buck Ratio, which quantifies the dollars earned by farmers for every donor dollar spent. Last I checked it was 15:1.[4] ROI can be measured for stakeholders in a number of different ways: by producing the same outcomes at a lower cost, by generating more results for the same cost, or by creating direct economic value to end beneficiaries.

• *Systemic change.* Today, some of the biggest (and most rewarding) investments in social change are focused on underlying "systemic" solutions (versus helping one individual at a time) by changing incentives, influencing public policy, creating public awareness, and building new institutions. A growing number of social investors and corporations are making high-profile bets on systemic solutions to such issues as education (such as charter schools and performance-based compensation); climate change (for example, new technologies, awareness campaigns, policy change); health care (for example, technology innovation, eradicating disease, access to insurance), and poverty in developing countries (such as inclusive markets strategies at the "bottom of the pyramid"). As the cost of these problems escalates geometrically, so too does the value of solving these problems at a systemic level. A 2010 report by the National Committee for Responsive Philanthropy found that for every dollar invested in advocacy, community-organizing, and civic-engagement activities of local groups in Washington, Oregon, Montana, and Idaho, the "return" was $150 in benefits such as wages, expanded services, state housing investments, and other programs. Committee Executive Director Aaron Dorfman said, "The true test of a philanthropy's success, in our view, boils down to this: Does their giving help stimulate real solutions and long-term results that actually touch the lives of people who need help."[5]

Here are a few examples that illustrate how nonprofits are achieving each of these three high-value outcomes.

## Change in Status

Status change is the ultimate aim of most human services. We don't just want to help someone do better in school; we want to change their status to "high school graduate." We don't just want to train someone with a set of skills; we want to change their status to "employed." We don't just want to provide a safe haven for battered women; we want to change their status to "independent." As I mentioned earlier, there are numerous ways to change a person's status, be it economic, social, physical, or intellectual status. The following are a few examples.

### United Way and Financial Self-Sufficiency

The United Way of Metropolitan Chicago (UWMC) funds hundreds of nonprofit agencies across the city. Many of these agencies help low-income people with financial issues, like getting and retaining a job or applying for tax credits and child-care subsidies. Although UWMC measured each of its grants individually, the agency was not in a position to answer questions from funders who wanted to know their impact on unemployment. All UWMC could capture was their contribution to different pieces of the overall problem: this many people trained in job skills at one nonprofit, that many people provided transportation to work by another nonprofit, and so on. The organization realized that in order to provide a more compelling answer, they would need to think about their impact differently. Chief Community Investment Officer Wendy DuBoe explains, "This is a situation where it's not as helpful to measure individual program output." Instead, she says, "We came up with a way to measure the change in people's overall financial condition and map out thresholds of progress."

Starting in 2009, UWMC began requiring that any agency receiving its funds use a new measurement framework. As a result, for the past funding cycle UWMC has been able to generate reports that synthesize the impact they've had on financial self-sufficiency across the Chicago area. For instance, every partner agency involved in financial services now measures job retention ninety days after job placement and calculates the amount of money garnered through public income supports like the Earned Income Tax Credit. "This way, we can add up results and aggregate our impact," says DuBoe. "When you're that broad and funding that many programs and need to get a handle on what you've accomplished, it makes a huge difference."

UWMC can now present to funders one big outcome that they are producing across the city: *increased financial self-sufficiency*. Their data shows that their programs are achieving results by moving people along a path from financial instability to economic sustainability (see Figure 5.1).

Focusing on a higher-value outcome (change in status from unstable to economically sustainable) has influenced not only what UWMC measures but also how it thinks about strategy. To really deliver on the outcome, UWMC is looking to create "community hubs" that integrate many types of programs under one roof. For example, located inside schools, these hubs will include financial resources for parents, afterschool programs for children, and other types of support for families. In this way UWMC could coordinate various services, reach a larger population, and deliver a greater outcome to the community. "The whole model changes," DuBoe explains. "UW is the largest funder of human services

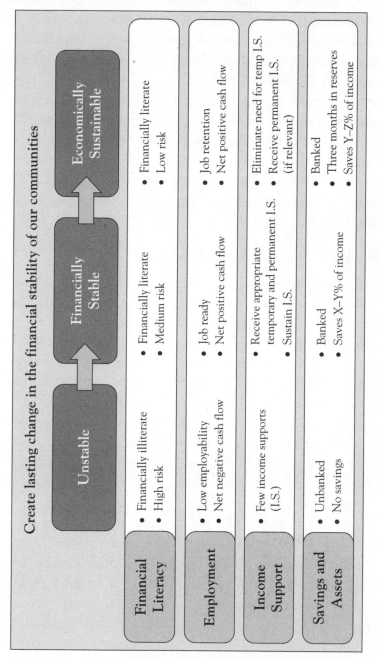

Figure 5.1. UWMC Financial Stability Presentation

after the government. Instead of taking our funding resources and underwriting a lot of individual programs—like, here's an afterschool sports program for kids, here's a program for adults to learn about the Earned Income Tax Credit—we use our funding to underwrite all those resources."

Other chapters of United Way are taking a similar tack, forging together multiple service offerings under one roof in order to produce higher value outcomes for the community. For example, United Way of Palm Beach County runs four Prosperity Centers in Florida that offer a one-stop source of services including vocational assistance, a home ownership program, free tax preparation, and benefits assistance.

### United Way of the Bay Area—SparkPoint Initiative

In 2009, United Way of the Bay Area (UWBA) launched SparkPoint Center in Oakland, California, a community hub designed for the working poor. The goal of the new center was to coordinate a wide variety of services and ensure that clients could continue to access help over longer periods of time. SparkPoint Oakland Coordinator Sharon Robinson explains, "It's a time when we want to think differently about service delivery. The old model hasn't met the needs for long-term sustainability and change." In an era of overwhelming job loss, home foreclosures, and high poverty rates in the San Francisco area, United Way wanted to find the most cost-effective way of delivering services that would make a lasting impact.

SparkPoint Center is doing something new—aiming for a higher-value outcome that changes the status of people in poverty. The model is based on a simple premise: bundling together two or more services results in greater economic progress for clients. UWBA estimates that two services bundled together are 65 percent more effective than just one, whereas three or more services are 85 percent more effective. The success rates are based on their clients' ability to achieve financial milestones in SparkPoint's three focus areas: increasing income, building assets, and reducing debt or improving credit.

For example, SparkPoint offers free tax help, job readiness training, and assistance applying for public benefits. The Center also offers education and counseling to help clients reduce debt, increase their credit scores, and avoid predatory lenders. In addition, the organization works one-on-one to help clients get "banked," through access to mainstream banking services, and build their savings, often working toward personal goals related to education or home ownership. SparkPoint staff members build relationships with clients and work with them over the course of several years to help them achieve their financial goals, offering a multitude of services along the way depending on the person's changing needs. In this way the SparkPoint Centers effectively address the underlying causes of the financial distress, rather than offering temporary fixes.

As the Center's Oakland Coordinator explains, the one-stop model is not a new concept. "What's new is that we work with folks in a more integrated, synergistic approach. It's not just about partners being co-located—it's about delivering in a more seamless way to our clients over a longer term." Clients and their families articulate long-term goals and work with a staff person to create and execute an action plan. For instance, one woman who recently used the center took on a number of challenges over a short period. She worked for seven months while increasing her credit score by ninety points. At the same time, she realized that she really wanted to go back to school, and the SparkPoint Center helped her with the process of getting into school and successfully applying for financial aid and income supports. SparkPoint staff also worked with her to get an eviction notice from her housing complex rescinded. In cases such as these, long-term relationships with clients are absolutely necessary to produce sustainable change. A three-month or even six-month program in credit counseling or job training would not have produced the same result. Real change takes time.

Equally important is the need to address a number of problems at once. SparkPoint assisted the woman in resolving her urgent housing and credit difficulties while attaining her long-term financial and educational goals. It is not unusual for a client to enter SparkPoint seeking one particular service, like help finding a job, and to wind up receiving immediate assistance in another area, like credit counseling and money management. The combination of services makes it much more likely that each client can achieve a sustainable improvement in his or her financial situation, because the root causes of the poverty are being addressed.

This success has allowed UWBA to reach out to a variety of stakeholders who value the outcome of financial self-sufficiency. The banking industry has been a key strategic partner because of its interest in offering more services to low-income people who are opening bank accounts for the first time. Industry events hosted by the local Federal Reserve Bank have fostered this collaboration between banks and the SparkPoint Initiative.

Local nonprofits, businesses, and public agencies are also impressed with the emphasis on higher-value outcomes and the fact that investing in SparkPoint Centers can produce sustainable results for the community. In the City of Oakland State of City address, Mayor Ronald Dellums cited SparkPoint Oakland as an important step to helping to build a more stable and safe community.[6] When meeting with Bay Area funders, UWBA consistently emphasizes its ability to produce lasting change—and ultimately to impact multiple generations of Oakland residents. By increasing the financial stability of parents, they note, they enable children to gain more opportunities to rise out of poverty themselves. Over time, investing in multiple services for struggling parents could yield significant positive results for the community. United Way of the Bay Area has a goal to cut the Bay Area poverty rate in half by 2020. Establishing SparkPoint Centers throughout the San Francisco Bay Area region is essential to achieving this goal.

## ROI

Return on investment or ROI is another high-value outcome. Funders want to know that their money is making a significant impact, and one way to do that is to show "bang for the buck." As I mentioned earlier, ROI can be measured for stakeholders in three ways: producing the same outcomes at a lower cost, generating more results for the same cost, or creating direct economic value to end beneficiaries. In these ways, funders can appreciate the value of the impact being produced. The following is an example of ROI.

### Committee on Institutional Cooperation: Producing a "Return on Collaboration"

The Committee on Institutional Cooperation (CIC), an educational nonprofit in the Midwest, is a consortium of the Big Ten universities plus the University of Chicago. The CIC's premise is simple: to develop collaborative programs in which each of the research universities can benefit by pooling their resources and sharing expertise. Collective purchasing and licensing agreements, for instance, save enormous amounts of money for each school and maximize faculty and student access to library resources and software programs. Shared courses save resources while offering more opportunities to students, particularly in the case of foreign languages—the consortium boasts 120 less commonly taught languages across all of its campuses. One of their most impressive projects is OmniPop, a fiber-optic network that allows researchers from different universities to easily collaborate, sharing massive datasets and collectively using bandwidth-intensive applications.

CIC is a fee-for-service based organization, with each university paying a flat membership fee and then individually determining how much it will invest in CIC services in a given year. CIC's leadership team recognized that with the economic downturn and corresponding budget freezes, it would be crucial to make a compelling case about the value they were providing to each school. "We quickly saw that the ability to articulate value back to the members was going to be critically important to maintaining their support over a number of years," says Barbara McFadden Allen, executive director. The staff also realized that they should involve the member schools throughout the measurement process. "We were quick to go to our stakeholders and say, 'What do you think is a value you get from the CIC, and how can we measure that?'" explains Allen. "And they told us, in no uncertain terms." The schools all valued the dollars they had saved, of course, but they also identified other important metrics that captured some of the less tangible results that CIC provided.

To showcase their impact, CIC then developed a Return on Collaboration metric: a calculation of inputs and outputs for each university in the consortium and for the organization as a whole (see Figure 5.2). Each school receives a report that captures its financial inputs to the CIC as well as other investments, such as faculty time spent at CIC meetings. "One thing we saw very clearly is campuses that put more in, get more out," notes Allen. Once the schools reviewed their Returns on Collaboration, they were driven to invest more in CIC programs. The universities have even taken the lead in identifying high-value future programs that they want CIC to launch and run. In sum, the process of measuring and sharing results has improved the relationship between CIC and the member schools. "It's enabled us to have a tighter connection with the campuses, so they really feel like they're partnering with us, and that made them trust us and increase their investment," says Allen.

Packaging impact as Return on Collaboration (a clever variation of Return on Investment) has had a tremendous effect on CIC's organizational funding. At the start of the last fiscal year, CIC knew they would be operating under a zero-percent budget increase due to the economic climate. Yet within a couple of weeks of the budget's approval, the campuses had already identified two new projects that they wanted to see, which effectively increased the budget by

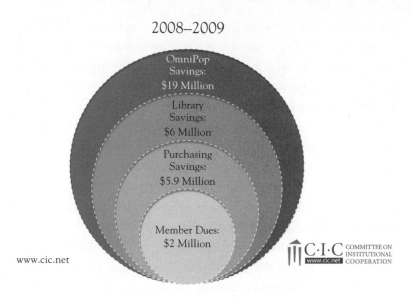

2008–2009

OmniPop
Savings:
$19 Million

Library
Savings:
$6 Million

Purchasing
Savings:
$5.9 Million

Member Dues:
$2 Million

www.cic.net

C·I·C  COMMITTEE ON
www.cic.net  INSTITUTIONAL
COOPERATION

**Figure 5.2.  CIC Return on Collaboration**

20 percent. "I don't think it would have happened if we weren't showing this Return on Collaboration and this value," says Allen.

## Systemic Change

Focusing on longer-term "systemic" solutions (versus short-term fixes) can offer funders a much greater return on their investment and create impact far beyond what any direct-service program can accomplish. Nonprofits can bring about systemic change in a number of ways; here is one example.

### Humane Society of the United States and Downed Cows

The Humane Society of the United States (HSUS) doesn't do what most people think it does. Most people's impression is that they run animal shelters and save pit bulls from the Michael Vicks of the world. Sort of. HSUS is a systemic player. They're not looking to change the world one dog at a time, but rather "to reduce suffering and to create meaningful social change for animals by advocating for sensible public policies, investigating cruelty and working to enforce existing laws, educating the public about animal issues, joining with corporations on behalf of animal-friendly policies, and conducting hands-on programs that make ours a more humane world."[7] In other words, the HSUS is all about systems change.

One of the biggest coups the HSUS ever pulled off took place in January 2008 at Hallmark Meat Packing in Chino, California. HSUS stationed an undercover investigator at the slaughterhouse, wearing a customized video camera under his clothes to obtain footage of injured or sick "downed" cows being slaughtered for meat production. The graphic video showed slaughter plant workers repeatedly kicking cows, ramming them with the blades of a forklift, jabbing them, and applying electrical shocks and other techniques to force sick or injured animals to walk to slaughter.[8] The video went viral, reaching tens of millions of people through just about every mainstream media outlet, from the *Wall Street Journal* to the *CBS Evening News*.

HSUS CEO Wayne Pacelle seized the moment to create a call to action: "This must serve as a five-alarm call to action for Congress and the U.S. Department of Agriculture. Our government simply must act quickly both to guarantee the most basic level of humane treatment for farm animals and to protect America's most vulnerable people, our children, needy families and the elderly from potentially dangerous food."[9] The evidence from the video was presented to then Agriculture Secretary Ed Schafer, and Pacelle urged the USDA to close a "loophole" that allows downed cattle to be slaughtered in rare cases and extend the ban to auction houses and other outlets.[10] After a review by the USDA, the department issued a total ban on downed cattle from the U.S. food supply to prevent the mistreatment of animals and ensure meat safety.[11]

This is just one example of how HSUS has been able to capitalize on high-profile media attention to mobilize its base, change public attitudes, and put animal rights issues at the forefront of the national agenda. HSUS has a powerful lobbying apparatus that operates in all fifty states. In the words of Andrew Rowan, the EVP of operations at HSUS, the organization is built around the concept of changing public attitudes toward animals and ultimately "to raise the status of animal issues in the marketplace of ideas, and our long-term influence on the way such issues are considered by public policy networks."[12]

HSUS measures its performance in a way that mirrors the organization's aspirations for system change. According to Beth Rosen, who led the evaluation efforts at HSUS: "An outcome for us means behavior change by a target group. The target group could be a corporation, a legislative body, a legal system, consumers, or animal advocates."[13] For HSUS, the ultimate impact was about the animals, but achieving the outcomes of changing the quality of life for animals depended on influencing the types of people who can change the condition of animals. Among its accomplishments in 2009, the HSUS claimed passage of 121 "pro-animal" state laws and the addition of 100 brands and companies to its fur-free list.

Any nonprofit organization, regardless of mission or scale, can achieve at least one of these high-value outcomes. Producing a status change, ROI, or systemic change is not unique to any one issue or any particular type of work. Every one of us is chasing at least one of these high-value outcomes, but we usually don't frame it this way.

Remember, marketing is about putting forth the best facet of your work and appealing to what your impact buyers really value. As nonprofits, we have to continue to refine our value propositions and, in this case, elevate them to meet the expectations of our market. That's what United Way, CIC, and HSUS have done. In some cases, such as that of United Way, that means reengineering program design to better produce high-value outcome. In other cases, such as inventing the phrase "return on collaboration," you're already producing high-value outcomes, but you need to find the right way to tell your story.

The following chapter will show you how you can elevate your organization's value proposition to produce higher-value outcomes.

# Chapter 6

# HOW TO INCREASE YOUR VALUE

The first element of "marketing your impact" is to identify your impact buyers and know what they value; the other part is to figure out how to produce that value! Typically, nonprofits think about value in the opposite way: we have an established set of activities or programs in place, often informed by research or past experience; then we call in marketing or development staff to help us tell our story. We approach measurement the same way: we bring in evaluators at the end of our work to measure and see what impact we produced. In both cases, we are approaching value as a default—a dependent variable that we cannot control. As a result, nonprofits often find that they can't make the case they really need to, to convince impact buyers, because they don't have compelling data or value propositions. In my experience, organizations usually face one of two issues when it comes to increasing their value: it's either a *messaging problem* or a *strategy problem*. Let's take a closer look at each, and I'll offer some examples and tips on how to overcome these challenges.

## Increasing Value Through Messaging

*Messaging* is the process of accurately and attractively describing your product (your impact) to your audience of impact buyers. It involves four elements: knowing your product well, knowing what you want to achieve (how you want your audience to respond), understanding what *drives* your customers to choose, and finally, figuring out how to describe your product in the terms that appeal to your customers' drivers and will motivate them to act.

Some nonprofits are doing super-high-value work—solving social problems, producing high-value outcomes. These organizations may in fact be producing real value for impact buyers, but the market doesn't understand or appreciate that value. In most cases, this is the result of either measuring the wrong things or communicating to the wrong stakeholders—or often both. Here's a typical example of a nonprofit's failure to convince impact buyers due to faulty messaging.

A professional fundraiser I know was hired by an organization to raise funds for a large public memorial pavilion honoring one of the city's founding fathers. The pavilion was to be located in a high-profile city park where the public could have free access and learn about the city's history. The fundraiser believed that one of the large retail insurance companies in town would be an ideal sponsor. When she approached the company's foundation, however, she was a bit taken aback by the questions they asked. They weren't so concerned with the pavilion itself, or what it stood for. They wanted to know, quite specifically, how many total visitors would see the exhibit every day, the specific demographics that would be reached, whether they would overlap with the company's target audience, and what percent of the company's target audience could be reached through the pavilion sponsorship. The fundraiser had no idea how to answer these sophisticated marketing questions, and she told the company as much. So the company reached out to its own internal marketing department to see if they could research these questions. The marketing team did some internal review and then told the foundation that they saw relatively little value in this opportunity. Still, the foundation cut a check to the organization for $250,000. When I asked the fundraiser why, she said it was because the CEO believed this aligned with his values for a "strong metropolis." Now here's the real kicker: I asked my friend what her original ask was to the company. "Two million," she said. Although $250,000 is great, the price of "I don't know" to this organization was a whopping $1.75 million! That's a marketing problem. In this case, the problem was the organization's lack of clarity about what really motivated the customer. Had they done some homework, they may have been able to figure out how to repackage their impact in a way that would appeal.

To understand how this issue can be remedied, let's look at a few more examples.

As you'll recall from our earlier discussion, Ronald McDonald House Charities has been creating valuable outcomes for the families it serves, and also for its impact buyers, namely hospitals. However, not all RMHs have had great success raising money from hospitals, despite the fact that more than 70 percent of children's hospitals are associated with an RMH program! Why is this? First off, the data that RMHs had been tracking was primarily related to activities, not outcomes (such as number of family stays, total dollars saved for families, satisfaction scores with stays at the House). Most RMHs weren't tracking key high-value outcome metrics that mattered to hospitals—for example, demonstrating that the patient satisfaction rates were significantly higher among RMH patients compared with the average, or that the length of stay for RMH patients was significantly shorter than the average. Second, RMHs weren't communicating their strongest messages to their impact buyers. Hospitals knew, intrinsically, that the RMHs were valuable, but few had any hard data to make the case. And when they did communicate with their hospitals, it was often more anecdotal in nature, with pictures and heartwarming stories of the children and families whose lives had been touched. Moreover, many of the RMHs were often approaching the wrong stakeholders at the hospitals—pitching their foundations for philanthropic grants, rather than approaching the business side of the hospital.

This was a classic messaging problem: the impact was there, but it wasn't being communicated to the right people in the right way.

RMHC faced the same challenge with another key impact buyer: McDonald's Corporation. In my interviews with the company and its franchisees (called "owner-operators"), there was high regard for RMHC and the work they did. But the value was primarily psychic. People felt RMHC was honoring the legacy of Ray Kroc to give back to the community, and they viewed the RMHs as iconic brands that created a "halo" for the business. Although the charity enjoyed significant support from the company, it was limited to the emotional appeal of its work. But once RMHC started to engage the corporation as an impact buyer—asking "How can we demonstrate the business value of our work?"—the business began to look at RMHC in a whole new way. RMHC began to discover new and more compelling ways that it could communicate its value to the business. Here are a few of that metrics that RMHC shared:

- Eight in ten Americans have a more positive image of companies that support a cause they care about.[1]

- Eighty-one percent of Americans are likely to switch brands, when price and quality are equal, to support a cause.[2]

- Sixty-six percent of Americans report having greater trust in those companies aligned with a social issue.[3]

- Ninety percent of workers whose company has a cause-related program feel proud of their company's values versus 56 percent of those whose employers are not committed to a cause.[4]

- Eighty-seven percent of employees of companies with cause programs feel a strong sense of loyalty to their company compared with 67 percent of those employed by companies without a cause association.[5]

- Eighty-two percent of respondents agree that
  a company's reputation for being a good corporate
  citizen would have some influence on whether or
  not they would buy or hold stock in a particular
  company.[6]

RMHC began to collect its own data, too. For example, through market research, the charity found that McDonald's customers who were aware of the charity were much more likely to revisit the stores. That was powerful, because "revisit intent" is a key indicator that the business tracks for itself. Moreover, RMHC encouraged the business to redesign crew uniforms to include an RMHC patch, to turn employees into brand ambassadors. And the charity began to position itself as a powerful branding and cause marketing partner for the business, measuring its contribution to key business metrics. Based on these changes, RMHC has garnered greater buy-in and investment from the company and from its owner-operators. Effectively, RMHC had figured out what motivated its impact buyers, then collected data (developed better information about its product) that demonstrated its delivery of the impact. The sale was a natural event after that.

The Committee on Institutional Cooperation (described in Chapter Five) is another case in point. What is so illustrative about the CIC is that they were able to dramatically increase their value to key impact buyers without changing any of their programs! The "return on collaboration" metric was simply a matter of cleverly restating their impact in terms that resonated. The phrase "return on collaboration" captured the value that they were *already* creating. CIC's member universities, who were true impact buyers, knew that they were getting value from the CIC; they just didn't know how much, nor did they have a way to describe it succinctly. Once the CIC quantified the return on investment—and mirrored it back to their members—the CIC saw an immediate bump in revenues. But there was an even more interesting phenomenon:

the members with the lowest ROI increased their investment too! Why? Because seeing the benchmarks for their peers helped them realize that they weren't putting enough faculty and staff time into the CIC programming to get the value they expected. In this way, better stating the value to impact buyers can not only increase money, it can also increase mission!

Here are a few of the key lessons learned on how you can use messaging to improve the value for impact buyers:

- *Don't ever assume.* Don't assume that your impact buyers know your value. If you don't know whether they do, they probably don't.

- *Speak their language.* The most compelling way to communicate to an impact buyer is to use their metrics and the language of their business. Figure out what they value most and show how you can move the needle.

- *Think in dollars and cents.* Money still talks, and to the extent that you can quantify the "ROI" of any investment in your outcomes, you'll be that much more convincing. Just make sure its credible and believable.

- *Communicate to convince, not justify.* Make your case at the front end, to build the business case for why impact buyers should invest in your outcomes. If you wait until the money is spent to communicate value, it sounds more like a justification.

## Increasing Value Through Strategy

Sometimes nonprofits are doing good work but not producing high-value outcomes. This is hard for some organizations to accept, as many are so emotionally attached to their work and believe in what they are doing. But this doesn't mean that your work isn't important or that you are not making a difference. It just means that if you want to be more compelling to influence buyers, you will need to find ways to push further along the value chain to produce higher levels of outcomes. This usually does not require rethinking an entire strategy or scrapping a program—it's more a matter of degree. The difference between ordinary outcomes and higher-value outcomes is typically a function of dosage, frequency, and duration. *Dosage* means the level of intensity of involvement (such as the amount of time someone spends in a program during a specified period). *Frequency* means how often someone participates (such as the number of times someone participates). And *duration* means how long someone stays involved (such as the number of months or years of involvement). Usually, when I come across organizations that don't meet the threshold for high-value outcomes, it's because their program involvement is too limited. A one-day volunteer event is not going to transform employees into "brand ambassadors." Reading a pamphlet is not likely to change someone's eating habits. It might; it's just not very likely.

Here's a typical example of a strategy problem. The executive director of a well-known afterschool program wanted to find a more compelling pitch for funders ("We want Gates money!" as she put it), so she hired an evaluator to come up with metrics to prove that her program was improving high school graduation rates. There was only one problem: the program primarily involved kids playing basketball after school. There was a study program, but few kids attended, and those that did mostly just did their homework. The issue wasn't a matter of measurement; the program simply wasn't designed to help kids graduate high school; it was primarily designed as a safe place for kids to stay off the streets and not get involved in gangs and drugs. Those were valuable outcomes in themselves. But they weren't the high-value outcomes that funders were looking for or that the executive director wanted to prove.

There are a number of ways that nonprofits can address the strategy challenge to produce a higher level of value for their impact buyers. In most cases, part of the puzzle is that nonprofits cling to old program strategies that weren't designed to produce the outcomes that the market values. Let's look at a few examples of how organizations have overcome this strategy problem to create more value for stakeholders.

Education outcomes are among the most desirable in the market for social change these days. But creating high-value educational outcomes is no easy trick. One of the organizations I advised specialized in youth study-abroad trips. The organization knew that their impact buyers were schools, in particular school district superintendents. But influencing these stakeholders wasn't easy. Superintendents were focused on hard-core student outcomes: student achievement and test scores, dropout rates, grade advancement, and graduation rates. To convince superintendents to support study-abroad trips, the organization wanted to be able to measure the impact of trips on student achievement. Wouldn't it be great to show that by studying abroad, students could do better in school? Or be more likely to go to college? But here was the problem: two or three weeks of studying history in Berlin is unlikely to change a student's academic performance. Simply put, the program was never designed to produce those types of outcomes. It was designed to teach students about the history of Germany and expose them to a different culture and way of life. But the focus, frequency, and duration of these programs are not sufficient to produce the high-value outcomes that superintendents value most.

There are two general ways to address this problem. One way is to change your strategy—or stretch it to create more value. For example, the study-abroad program could be expanded to include a pre-trip curriculum that involved a semester of research and classroom learning and a post-trip internship with a local firm that does business abroad. Moreover, an eligibility requirement could be put in place that required a certain level of academic performance (or improvement) in order to participate in the study-abroad program. This more comprehensive design would be more likely to change a student's status academically, or influence the student's long-term career plans.

The other way to address the strategy problem is to size your outcomes more appropriately for your program. For example, it could be possible to show that the trip changed a student's attitudes about certain people, or inspired a student to pursue further study in a foreign language. These outcomes are more reasonably related to the activity.

A final case example illustrates the point that sometimes non-profit leaders need to have the courage to actually redefine their mission to achieve a high-value outcome. This particular case study is excerpted from the book *The Power of Social Innovation* by Stephen Goldsmith:

> Anyone who believes that entrepreneurship cannot occur inside government should meet New York City Deputy Mayor Linda Gibbs. In 2002, with more than 33,000 homeless people in New York City, Mayer Bloomberg appointed Gibbs as commissioner of homeless services. New York City's Emergency Assistance Unit, a make-shift stop for homeless families without shelter placement, was overflowing. People slept on floors. Gibbs noted that the Department of Homeless Services (DHS) had made shelters its centerpiece, which perversely perpetuated chronic homelessness rather than reducing it. As Gibbs later observed, "We were smart enough to know how to help the clients' underlying needs. But you put them in the shelters and suddenly the shelters became the solution, which is turning the world upside down." With Bloomberg's backing, Gibbs redefined the agency's goal from serving the homeless to ending homelessness. This step forced the DHS to take preventative actions before things got worse. The agency shifted its focus from supposedly temporary, stop-gap shelter to permanent housing with supports. After conducting research on the underlying causes of homelessness, Gibbs launched a new program called "Homebase," which was designed to address

three main goals: 1) preventing homelessness; 2) helping families find immediate alternatives to temporary shelter or, failing that, shortening their time in shelters; and 3) preventing repeated stays. Homebase also provided clothes for job interviews, funded job training, and secured child care, mental health care, education and employment services. The impact on the families and communities served was significant. By July 2008, more than 90 percent of the 10,042 households served by Homebase had stayed out of shelters for a year after being served.[7]

In this case, it took nothing short of a complete program redesign to produce the high-value outcome of changing the status of homeless people. Tinkering around the edges of the current program simply wouldn't have produced this level of impact.

Here are some tips on how to "stretch" your program or strategy to create greater value:

1. *Extend.* One way to improve the value of your strategy is to extend the scope of your intervention to reach next-level outcomes. Food banks can achieve a high-value outcome by registering eligible families for SNAP in addition to feeding them meals. Afterschool programs can add an academic component to influence the high-value outcome of lowering the dropout rate. Job training programs can include job placement services to reach the high-value outcome of employment.

2. *Innovate.* It's not always about doing more. Some organizations can create high-value outcomes just by using some creativity. Urban Gateways (the Chicago nonprofit focused on bringing arts to children in underserved communities, profiled in Chapter Four) innovated by connecting its current programs to a new context (community development) to influence systemic change.

3. *Partner.* An easy way to increase your value is by partnering with others to jointly produce high-value outcomes. That's

how United Way's prosperity centers are able to deliver status change, instead of just providing one-off services.

4. *Right-size*. Finally, you can always just aim at less ambitious outcomes. Sometimes the best way to realize more value is to find more impact buyers for the outcomes you are already producing rather than trying to stretch to a "bigger" outcome. For example, there are many impact buyers who have lots of money to invest in changing kids' status from "at-risk" to "positive development"—it doesn't always have to be about graduation rates!

At the end of the day, marketing your impact is about connecting your outcomes to the market in ways that create value for stakeholders. The core concept here is "value." Value is what creates leverage and what triggers funding. But value is completely relative. Think of the expression *One man's trash is another man's treasure*. Amazingly, with the exception of New York City's Department of Homeless Services, every organization cited in this chapter was *already producing value* without having to change anything they were doing. It is just a matter of marketing—connecting your outcomes to the market by tapping into a new set of stakeholders who value what you are doing and are willing to pay.

We've reached the end of this chapter and of Part Two. You have learned that in the social capital market, the key is *value*. It's not that psychic benefits aren't important—it's just that when you seek customers who value your impact, you enter a new, much larger market. To succeed in that world, you'll need to follow new rules. First, you'll need to recognize that there *are* customers willing to pay for what you do. Then you'll need to focus on the highest-value outcomes for your work. Finally, you will need to increase your value to reach the point where potential customers are motivated to buy. This, of course, is *marketing*.

Now that we've learned how to *market* our impact, let's take the final step and learn how to tap into a new stream of financial resources by *selling* our impact—the topic of Part Three.

# Part III

## SELLING YOUR IMPACT

### Creating and Closing Deals in the Social Capital Market

**Key Takeaways**

- Your need to sell versus the customer's need to buy

- Moving from values to value propositions

- Creating the business case

- How to close the deal

*Selling your impact* is about moving from the ask to the answer. In the social capital market, we are not asking for a contribution; rather, we are answering a need. The best sales people don't push their products; they solve customer problems. That's not been our traditional orientation in the nonprofit sector—after all, we're the ones with the problems! But the social capital market has put us in a position to help others—government agencies, corporations, service providers, and beneficiaries themselves—who value what we can offer them. Selling is about showing these prospective impact buyers how we can address their critical needs and create value.

In Part Two we learned how to package outcomes in a way that the market will buy. In Part Three, you will learn how to convince prospective impact buyers to purchase your outcomes. This part is based on my experience working closely with many different funders, understanding how they work and how they make decisions in today's environment. In Chapter Seven, you'll learn the true meaning of "it's not about you"—that is, you'll come to understand that successful sales people learn to listen to and solve their customers' problems. In Chapter Eight, you'll learn how to approach an organization that can benefit from your social impact, pitch your product to them, and close the deal. Chapter Nine sums up these lessons in seven memorable laws—rules you can rely on to guide you through any deal.

# Chapter 7

# IT'S NOT ABOUT YOU, IT'S ABOUT THEM

To successfully sell in the social capital market, the first thing you need to do is forget everything you know about fundraising. Classic fundraising is designed around a totally different proposition: *Let me explain why we are worthy of your contribution ... We are doing amazing work ... Our programs are recognized by XYZ agencies ... We partner with the most prestigious whoever ... Our executive director is respected nationally for A, B, C ... Our programs serve thousands of YYY demographic.* We explain what we do. We appeal to compassion. We use powerful anecdotes. We underline the need. We ingratiate ourselves. We demonstrate our accountability. In short: it's all about *us* (meaning our organization and our worthy beneficiaries). And for a psychic benefit donor, that is exactly the right approach.

But that's not the right approach for an impact buyer. To illustrate why this is so, let me tell you what happened (true story) to a young executive director for a youth development organization during a fundraising pitch he made this year to a $15 billion telecommunications company. The executive director was told he had ten minutes to make his presentation to the company's CEO, and that the presentation should be "very focused and speak the corporation's language and focus on the proposition, model, and benefits." Here's what the charity presented:

- *Slide 1: Why Us:* We reach millions of people, we have multifaceted programs, we are innovative, we have low overhead, we've garnered lots of media attention, and we've won many awards.

- *Slide 2: How Our Model Works:* We work through schools to implement our program and give youth new opportunities for social engagement.

- *Slide 3: Our Impact:* There are various benefits our program can offer to local communities and to the beneficiaries we serve.

- *Slide 4: Proposed Program Model:* We will bring our standard program to your community.

- *Slide 5: How We Can Leverage Your Business:* Your employees and their families can volunteer to help us in several different ways.

- *Slide 6: Benefits to Your Business:* Our program will help engage youth in your community, including children of employees. We will feature your logo at our events, in our program materials, and on our website.

- *Slide 7: Cost to Your Business:* We would like you to contribute $1.75 million per year for three years.

- *Slide 8: How to Move Forward:* Here are the steps you'll need to take to approve this contribution

The CEO listened intently for five minutes, then lost interest and started flipping through the printed copy of the presentation. At fifteen minutes, he stopped the presentation. The CEO then proceeded to tell the young executive that he had no interest in the fluff or the accomplishments or background of the organization. The executive later recalled the CEO's reaction: "He said we needed to have a clear, focused pitch on what we were going to do for *them*, how they would benefit, and how they could scale this project going forward. Bottom line, he felt that our presentation focused too much on us, and not enough on them, and the value propositions for their company."

What can we learn from this story?

First, fundraising is all about the proposition. If your proposition is emotional, then it *is* about you, your work, and how what you do matters to the people you are soliciting. If your proposition is based on value, then it's about what needs you can meet, the value you can offer, and why that matters to the people you're soliciting. Those are the only two propositions, with subtle variations, that you can make. In this example of the youth organization, the CEO wanted to hear a value-based proposition, but the executive used an emotive pitch. The presentation did not focus on the company's real needs or pain; instead it focused entirely on the charity's needs and what the company could offer them.

Second, if you're making your pitch based on value, the value must be compelling. Too many nonprofits make half-hearted propositions that are really just emotional pleas dressed up as value (such as when nonprofits offer companies the value of printing their corporate logo on a banner at a charity event—the branding value is negligible; it's just a nice gesture). Nonprofits do a great job of talking about the value *they* will receive—how, for example, companies can loan them executives, or how the funding will benefit the charity. But when it comes to convincingly showing the value to the other party, we often gloss over the details and make throw-away statements like "this is a great opportunity to engage your employees" or "supporting us will improve your reputation." If you're making a value-based pitch, it must be substantiated and measurable. In the case of the youth organization cited above, the value proffered to the corporation was insubstantial, and not clearly articulated.

Third, your effort should be commensurate with your ask. If you're asking for millions of dollars, you should invest a hundred thousand dollars' worth of effort! Not literally, of course. But it should feel like it. Your presentation is an investment, and you often have just one bite at the apple. That doesn't just mean fancy graphics or a laminated cover. It means that the thought-work that you invest in researching the prospective donor, crafting the value proposition, and creating the presentation should be *substantial*. It's not unheard of to spend a month or two preparing for a major pitch. In the case just cited, the youth organization should have read everything they could get their hands on about the telecommunications firm—their Form 10-Ks, annual reports, media coverage, analyst reports, CEO speeches, and so on. From this research and other interviews, the organization could determine the company's key growth markets, customer segments, pain points, revenue sources, employee issues, and CSR problems. This should have been used to form the basis for the charity's value proposition.

The "it's not about you, it's about them" theory is not new in the world of sales. Consider this bit of advice from a seasoned sales executive:

> All sales people, today, sell solutions. At least that's what most sales people say they are doing. If sales people are really acting consultatively, selling solutions, why are so many customers sick of sales pitches?
>
> We hear customers saying:
>
> - They (the sales people) always come in here pitching their latest products and technologies without telling me how it solves our problems.
> - They say they have solutions before they even know my problems.
> - The sales person doesn't understand my business.
> - They tell me about the products; I have to figure out whether it will solve my problems!
> - They just want to push their products without understanding our needs!

Most sales people focus on their need to sell, not their customer's need to buy. Putting the customer first in the selling process is simple, yet enables sales people to achieve real success. It enhances the sales person's relationships with their customer. It enables them to clearly demonstrate their value. Finally, it is key to competitive success![1]

Sound familiar?

Assuming you are making a value-based pitch to an impact buyer, how do you make it about them? How do you sell a "solution?" There are two key elements: (1) know your customer and their need to buy, and (2) know what you have to offer and how it can create value for your customer.

## Identifying the Need to Buy

To effectively sell your impact, you have to know your customo-mer. To know your customer does not mean to know your customer personally or to be familiar with their organization. It means to *really* know your customer—their business, their strengths and weaknesses, their needs, their business objectives, who they serve as customers or constituents, how their economics work, and so on. Most important, you must know their pain—where they have real needs, needs so significant that the organization or individual is willing to part with its precious few resources in order to solve them. And you must also know their opportunity, meaning how the entity produces value—that is, either generates revenue or grows. Solving pain or creating opportunity are the keys to creating leverage. Nothing less. And by customers, I'm referring not just to corporations, but also to *any* impact buyers. Remember that an impact buyer is someone with an ability to pay, clear outcomes, and a high level of value associated with those outcomes.

There are many prospective donors who don't have any real needs. They may just be nice people who express an interest in your work, but there is nothing of real value that you can offer them. Those people are not impact buyers. If there is no pain or no compelling opportunity, then there is no leverage and no sale. *Need* is the ultimate litmus test to differentiate between a mere stakeholder and an impact buyer. Here's how the for-profit world defines *customer need to buy*: "All customers have goals and objectives. The customer need to buy is the result of business problems, opportunities or 'pain' influencing their ability to achieve their goals or objectives."[2]

So how do you determine an impact buyer's need to buy? Each impact buyer is unique, with a unique set of circumstances, business drivers, opportunities, and needs. Here are some of the general questions that you'll want to answer about each impact buyer:

- *How do they make money?* Every organization makes money—corporations, nonprofits, government agencies, even individuals. It is critical to understand the levers that influence the flow of funds to the organization (for example, is it from consumers, other companies, government, a few big donors?). Moreover, you should also know which products, services, or programs are the biggest or most lucrative. This will help you to sharpen your picture of their need to buy.

- *Which social outcomes matter the most?* Many organizations will rattle off a long list, but there are always one or two key outcomes that really matter. Sometimes outcomes matter because of internal priorities, sometimes they pose a risk to the organization, and sometimes they are critical for that organization's oversight, compliance, or funding. For example, schools may be under more pressure to influence student achievement outcomes than attendance or teacher satisfaction.

- *How do they measure success?* Knowing the metrics that *really* matter to the organization (or department or individual) is critical to your ability to create influence. There are usually only a few that really matter. One is likely to be a financial metric, and the nature of metric can be very important: for example, an organization that is focused on absolute revenue growth may behave very differently from one that is focused on net profitability. You should also know the frequency that the metric is reported and to whom (board, investors, the public). In Chapter Six I presented the example of Ronald McDonald House Charities: it was critical to know that the company paid attention to "customer revisit intent" as a key indicator. Similarly, knowing that hospitals care about length of stay allowed RMHC to focus on that metric as a leverage point.

• *What is the decision maker's personal win?* The decision whether to fund a project is often made by an individual, and that person is human—with an ego, ambitions, fears, and a personal agenda. Knowing this is essential to creating leverage. For example, one program officer at a foundation I advised loved getting media attention—he was particularly predisposed to high-profile projects that would get a lot of press. Knowing that was important to emphasize in the need to buy. People that are up for a promotion may be particularly risk-averse; others may be looking to make their mark. Everyone has a personal win; to create leverage, you'll need to figure out what motivates your decision maker.

• *What are the current hot-button issues?* Every organization (and individual) has issues of the day and controversies. These aren't always negative. For example, one funder had just been defrauded of millions of dollars in its Africa bureau. Knowing this would be especially important if you were pitching an international project. In another case, a corporation had just completed a huge merger, making HR issues a top priority for the organization. That might be good to know if you're proposing a volunteering or employee engagement opportunity. An individual may be changing careers and therefore more likely to pay for a particular type of job training or networking opportunity. Knowing what's going on inside gives you further insight into the buyer's need.

• *What makes the CEO (or top leader) tick?* People are by nature idiosyncratic. And money is necessarily political. So whether you're pitching a government agency, a corporation, or a large nonprofit, you need to know the CEO's personality and passions—what gets him or her excited. This is the person that can usually make or break your success with an organization, and if you can appeal to the CEO's personal agenda, you are more likely to get what you want.

• *What is their Achilles heel?* Every organization has some major weakness that isn't always obvious. For some large corporations it may be their reputation. For other organizations it may be an overreliance on one source of funding. Knowing this information can be critical to increasing your leverage.

• *Who are their key influencers?* Most organizations (and individuals) have external influencers that hold significant sway over their decision making. Some individuals do what their close friends do. Others follow celebrities or other respected members of the community. The same applies to organizations. Some funders follow *certain* other funders (I've heard many say that foundations can be like "lemmings following each other off a cliff"). One corporate foundation I advised had an external advisory board that was highly influential due to the technical nature of some of its grant making. Any information you can find out about who these key influencers are and how they think (and who influences *them!*) will increase your leverage.

Keep in mind that these questions work only if the prospective impact buyer has some pain or some upside potential. If this is a purely psychic decision (with no value exchange), leverage will not work. For example, many family foundations have no needs or upside—they just give away money to people they like. So trying to determine need is futile. Still, some foundations (social investors) are more outcomes-driven and do have resources directly tied to the achievement of outcomes. These social investors have a mandated need to buy certain outcomes. The same goes for some government agencies and some federal and state initiatives, in which case the pain is congressional oversight or compliance with the law that requires that certain outcomes be achieved.

To fully answer the "need to buy" questions, you'll need to access much better information than what is publicly available. Most of the data we traditionally seek out about prospects is fairly routine and cursory (biographical information, financial data, public initiatives). Most of the data sources we use are sufficient for these needs—donor databases, foundation websites, 990 tax returns, blogs, internet searches, and the like. This routine type of information may be enough to establish an affinity with a potential impact buyer, but it's not enough to determine the buyer's need or pain. You'll need to dig a lot deeper. Here are some tips:

- Study annual reports, analyst reports, industry studies.

- Read their press releases, product brochures, and sales literature.

- Read the trade magazines and press representing their industries.

- Talk to people you know inside the organization.

- Read media accounts and press, both positive and negative.

- Read or watch speeches by the CEO and other executives.

- Interview any partners, customers, employees, grantees, or other people affiliated with the organization that you can get to know.

- Take a close look at the organization's financial statements.

Once you've identified the need to buy, the logical next question is, what do you have to offer to help the impact buyer solve the pain or to create new value?

## Articulating Your Value Proposition

Eventually, selling your impact does become about you. But it's not the "about you" that most of us are used to talking about. We typically try to impress impact buyers with our organization's credentials, our awards, our prestigious donors or funders, our evaluations, our board, our track record of success, our innovative programs, and more. But that's just describing who you are. Value propositions are those things about you that are going to fulfill the customer's need to buy. Value propositions are the direct, tangible results or benefits that your programs, efforts, or services can deliver to an impact buyer. There is robust literature about how to develop value propositions, and even consultants who specialize in doing just that—but we don't need to overcomplicate this. For purposes of selling your impact, we just have to be able to explain the tangible, quantifiable benefits to the impact buyer that we can deliver.

Most of us don't have a lot of experience developing value propositions. In fact, the whole concept of a value proposition as a benefit to a customer makes little sense in the nonprofit world. That's because most of our stakeholders lack a need to buy. Those whom we consider to be customers—our beneficiaries—have no ability to pay. So there's clearly no point in trying to convince them to take something for free! On the other hand, our funders (whom we also consider to be customers) do have the ability to pay, but they do not consume our services. It's almost impossible to try to convince someone to pay for a product or service that offers them nothing in return (beyond good feelings). And therein lays the crux of the problem. But the social capital market offers a way out of this existential dilemma. In this new world we entertain a whole new set of customers—impact buyers who can both consume *and* pay for our social impact. With a monocular focus on one unified customer, we can more clearly articulate what we have to offer and how that customer stands to benefit.

Here are the key criteria for a strong value proposition:

- Clearly states the value or benefits (both tangible and measurable)

- Attuned to the needs of the buyer (addresses either their pain or the potential upside)

- Differentiates from competitors (based on value or level of impact)

- Gives a reason to believe (such as track record, success stories)

- Speaks the language of the buyer

One of the most challenging elements of the value proposition for nonprofits is the concept of competitive differentiation. First, we don't like to think of ourselves as competing with each other—the whole concept is anathema to the collaborative nature of nonprofit work. Second, we don't really have a way to compare ourselves to competitors because we define our work by what we do, not by the value we create. But when we convert our work into outcomes, and we link those outcomes with impact buyers who value them, competitive differentiation becomes a powerful component of our value proposition. This is a constructive, informative way to talk about our work, and it does not have to threaten the ethos of the sector.

Take the House Theatre in Chicago, for example (full disclosure: the author is a board member). The House is a tiny theatre (under $500,000 in revenues) that writes all of its own original plays. There's lots of competition: close to two hundred theatres in Chicago, including the famed Steppenwolf Theatre, the Chicago Shakespeare Theater, and the Goodman Theatre. However, in 2008, thirty-six thousand people saw a House production—a greater total audience than is enjoyed by almost any other theater in the city! The House Theatre—with seventeen premieres in six years, twenty-three positive reviews by theater critics, and oodles of awards—had an average cost per person served of $21.52. Compare this with other, larger theaters, which won less critical acclaim and reached audiences at a cost of $125–$150 per person served. The House used this information to strengthen its value proposition to *beneficiaries that can pay, social investors,* and other impact buyers in Chicago.

Language is critical to value propositions. Impact buyers speak diverse languages, and if you want to be persuasive you have to translate your persuasion points into words that make sense to each impact buyer. For example, at a company I advised, which was in the midst of a turnaround, the CSR director made a presentation to the senior leadership team. He bragged that the firm had reached a hundred thousand employee volunteer hours. Rather than patting him on the back or even smiling, the CEO noted, "That just sounds like a hundred thousand hours that people aren't working!" Companies don't think in terms of volunteering hours; they think in terms of employee engagement, employee satisfaction, and employee retention. The same is true for other organizations. Hospitals think in terms of patient outcomes, bed occupancy rates, length of stay, reimbursement rates, and patient satisfaction. Educators think in terms of graduation rates, grade advancement, test scores, school culture, teacher quality, college access, and the like. Make sure you do your homework to understand the language of the impact buyer you are selling to, and to translate your value into terms that are meaningful to them.

Note that value propositions are not the same as outcomes. *Outcomes* are the changes or results produced by your work. *Value propositions* are the ways in which those changes can benefit an impact buyer. So in effect, a value proposition is what links your outcome to the social capital market. It translates the value or benefits of your work into an attractive proposition for the impact buyer. Value propositions answer the ultimate "so what?" question.

Here are a few examples of how a value proposition can be expressed:

> *Youth empowerment organization.* This organization provides community service opportunities for students and helps them develop leadership skills. Figure 7.1 illustrates its value proposition to schools, which are asked to invest in some of its activities.

| Your Program or Service | The School's Need to Buy | Value Proposition to the School |
|---|---|---|
| • Specialized educational materials<br>• Volunteering opportunities<br>• Leadership training<br>• Peer support networks | • Some schools have mandatory service requirements and don't have a way to fulfill them.<br>• Poor reputation can limit enrollment and decrease funding which depends on enrollment.<br>• Performance-based funding for teachers is tied to student achievement. | • Schools attract more students (and funding) due to publicity and enhanced reputation.<br>• Social engagement and leadership opportunities help low-performing students excel and high-performing students deliver even higher performance. |

**Figure 7.1. Youth Empowerment Organization Value Proposition**

| Your Program or Service | The Hospital's Need to Buy | Value Proposition to the Hospital |
|---|---|---|
| • RMH overnight guest rooms<br>• Support groups for families<br>• Access to medical information<br>• Free meals | • Low patient satisfaction<br>• Patients not using hospital due to travel/housing costs for families<br>• Longer stays occupying beds that could be better utilized<br>• Low adherence to outpatient treatment for nonlocal patients | • Ability to attract new patients who otherwise wouldn't come to hospital<br>• Higher than average patient and doctor satisfaction scores<br>• Faster turnover of beds, leading to more revenues<br>• RMH proximity, improving adherence to treatment |

**Figure 7.2. Ronald McDonald House Charities Value Proposition**

*Ronald McDonald House Charities.* RMHC provides a home away from home by offering a nearby place for families to stay when children are in the hospital. The example (Figure 7.2) illustrates their value proposition to hospitals.

You should develop a separate value chain for impact buyer, and then validate them through direct engagement with those stakeholders. The blank form (Figure 7.3) can serve as a template.

Finally, one hidden element embedded in every value proposition is a *reverse* value proposition: what the impact buyer has to offer *you*. Impact buyers want to believe that they can provide extra-financial value to a nonprofit—value beyond their cash investment. There is still a significant feel-good factor to any dealings with a nonprofit—this reality is undeniable. Therefore

| Your Program or Service | The Need to Buy | Value Proposition |
|---|---|---|
|  |  |  |

**Figure 7.3. Value Proposition Template**

making people feel good about their contribution to your mission is still an essential part of the overall value equation. Articulating the *reverse* value proposition (such as additional expertise, the legitimizing halo of an established brand, in-kind contributions) makes the entire value exchange more appealing to an impact buyer. In effect, this turns the *reverse* value proposition into a value proposition itself!

Now that we've mastered the key concepts of selling, let's put it all together and create the pitch. That is the subject of our next chapter.

# Chapter 8

# THE ART OF THE DEAL

A friend once told me "There are fifty ways of doing things; ten of them are right. Just make sure you are doing one of the ten. And never argue between numbers seven and eight." Making a successful pitch is an art form. There is no single prescription, but there are some universal truths. There is no standard choreography, but there is a critical path. And there aren't any magic words, but there is a formula.

The good news is that you are now armed with a potent weapon that few nonprofits ever get to use—leverage! The mere fact that you have something that someone else wants is power in itself, regardless of how you deploy it. In many cases, just getting in front of the right people (impact buyers) is enough to improve your results in fundraising. That said, how you get to those people, and what you say once you're there, matters a lot and can make or break your chances of getting funded.

I've sat on both sides of these conversations. For years I've worked with some of the most influential foundations, donors, corporations, and governments, advising them on how to "buy" the social impact they need and how to get better results for their money. So I've seen how impact buyers make their decisions. I've heard their debates. I've reviewed their data. I've followed their logic. I've prepared their internal reports. Nothing I will share here reveals any trade secrets or confidential information. Rather, these are merely my insights and observations about how decisions get made on the inside, behind the closed doors.

I've also advised many of the world's leading nonprofit organizations, social entrepreneurs, and international NGOs on how to measure and sell their impact. I've developed their success equations. I've evaluated their impact. I've helped them prepare their grant applications. I've seen their pitfalls. And I've coached them on their interactions with impact buyers. It has become glaringly obvious what works—and what doesn't.

I'm assuming by now you've done your homework:

- You know your impact.

- You've identified your impact buyers.

- You've analyzed their need to buy.

- You've clearly defined your value propositions.

The obvious question, then, is how do you package all this up and sell it? Or to put it more bluntly, how do you get the money? The strategy for selling your impact has five key steps:

1. Find a "first friend" or a champion inside.
2. Map out your strategy.
3. Locate the "buckets" of money.
4. Build the business case.
5. Overcome channels of resistance.

## Step 1: Find a "First Friend" or a Champion Inside

When I founded my first nonprofit (the Center for What Works), I had a tough time attracting board members. No one with a big name wanted to join until someone else did. You know the drill.

And then I had the good fortune to meet with Knight Kiplinger. Knight is editor-in-chief of *Kiplinger's Personal Finance* magazine, the Kiplinger Letter, and Kiplinger.com. I explained what we did and how I thought we could make a huge impact in the world. And then I asked Knight if he'd be willing to serving on our advisory board. He asked me who else was on the board, and I sheepishly told him "No one." The way he responded wasn't what I had expected. He said "Well, you know what you need, Jason? You need a 'first friend.' Someone who will step up so that others will feel more comfortable joining. Count me in!"

Finding your first friend will give you a huge leg up in attracting other impact buyers. One of the biggest challenges you'll face in approaching any organization or potential investor is merely getting in the door. A first friend can help introduce you to other impact buyers and intermediaries (who can then introduce you to other impact buyers). But a first friend also helps in another way: he or she can mitigate the risk for other potential investors to whom you are an unknown quantity. When you look for impact buyers, you don't want to just look for someone to invest in your outcomes; you want to also look for someone who can also invest in your organization's success.

Another version of a first friend is an "organizational champion." A champion is someone who sees the value in what you do and is willing to advocate on your behalf inside an organization or to a third party. This person doesn't have to be powerful but should know the ropes and be willing to help. You will rarely succeed in pitching a large impact buyer without a champion. The champion will be your friend on the inside, a source of intelligence who can explain how the organization works and teach you how to navigate the red tape. Finding a champion is a function of meeting enough people until you find one that gets your value proposition—or at least is willing to help you refine it. You'll want to use every affinity you have—board members, friends, family, alumni of your college,

fraternity members (Knight Kiplinger was one of mine!), cowork-
ers, and casual acquaintances—to help you find your champion at
a particular organization. One nonprofit I worked with found their
champion at a foundation through an employee who rode the train
every day with a foundation employee!

## Step 2: Map Out Your Strategy

The complex impact buyer is like a Rubik's Cube: you have to
keep turning it different ways until it clicks. The points of entry
aren't usually obvious, and the strategy for how to get to the right
decision makers is rarely straightforward. Your champion can help
you avoid spinning wheels and identify the best way to position
your organization vis-à-vis the impact buyer's needs. Here are the
key elements of strategy you'll need to figure out:

- *Who are the decision makers?* The first thing you need to
  know is who writes the check. I know organizations that have
  spent months trying to get in front of people who don't have
  the power to make a funding decision. Once you've identified
  the decision makers, you'll need to determine their priorities
  and personal agenda. What are they looking to accomplish
  within the organization or within their career? What pressures
  are they under? In effect, you're looking for their personal need
  to buy.

- *Where is the sweet spot?* Your champion can help you figure
  out the real needs within the organization. What do they
  value most right now? For example, a company that just
  completed a merger will have much more pressing HR needs
  than a mature company that is trying to enter a new market.
  Foundations are the same. What is publicly on their website is
  not always what really matters on the inside. For example, the
  CEO of one foundation I advised was interested in funding

only systemic approaches to education reform, even though the website said that they funded student achievement and teacher training programs. Another funder was in a spend-down mode and was interested in only large, national projects where they could invest a lot of capital. The writing isn't always on the wall, as it were.

- *What are the biggest hurdles?* Your champion can also educate you about the key obstacles and roadblocks you're likely to encounter. Again, few of these will be obvious to the casual observer. These could be anything, even the not-so-obvious: one foundation had a board member who got declined for a Bank of America credit card and refused to approve any partnership involving that organization! More common obstacles include timing, budgets, related decisions, personalities involved, impending policies, and political considerations.

- *What's the precedent?* History is often the key to predicting the future for many large-impact buyers. It's always easier to get something done if they've done something like this before. This could be similar grants that a foundation has given, similar partnerships for an intermediary, or similar types of sponsorships that a company has underwritten. If there is no precedent, it doesn't mean that the proposition is impossible, it just means that it's a lot harder. The best way to hedge your risk if you're proposing something new is to find an analogous deal in the past or a way to relate your project to something else the organization routinely does.

## Step 3: Locate the Buckets of Money

This is always the $64 million question: "Where's the money?" Finding eligible funding for a project within an organization is always the biggest challenge and requires the most creativity. Let's just get this out of the way now: no one ever has money—no company, no government, no foundation, no intermediary! The first answer you'll always hear, no matter how compelling your value proposition, is "We don't have a lot of money for this type of thing." Money is never just lying around in slush funds. Funding is always stored in buckets—predetermined budget categories—and most of that is "already allocated." So the first step is to understand where those buckets are, what's available in each, and who controls the budget for each. It is also important to know when the buckets replenish (such as when the fiscal year ends).

The key is to persevere until you find the right bucket—do not give up after the first few tries! For example, one charity pitched the community affairs department at a large company to purchase educational materials and charity-sponsored apparel as rewards for company employees. Alas, the department had no budget for this type of use. But the human resources department did (there was a bucket for "employee incentives" that could be spent on corporate gifts, but no one had considered using it for charitable corporate gifts like these before). Another case in point: one nonprofit I worked with approached an impact buyer to fund technical assistance for its affiliates. The impact buyer told the nonprofit unequivocally that the organization didn't have any money to invest in capacity building. But with a bit of probing (and help of an internal champion), the nonprofit discovered a training budget that hadn't been used and was more than sufficient to cover the costs. The bottom line: there's almost always money somewhere if the value proposition is compelling enough.

## Step 4: Build the Business Case

Most nonprofits are familiar with the concept of "a case for support," which is a philanthropic justification for funding the organization. The Association of Fundraising Professionals (AFP) defines a case for support as "the reasons why an organization both needs and merits philanthropic support, usually by outlining the organization's programs, current needs, and plans."[1] Some have also referred to a case for support as "an encyclopedic accumulation of information about the organization, its cause, and how it serves its cause."[2]

According to the AFP, the components of a case are as follows:

- Mission

- Vision

- History

- Statement of community problem

- Goals of the campaign

- Objectives to meet these goals

- Programs and services

- Staffing

- Governance

- Facility needs

- Endowment

- Budget for the campaign

- Statement of needs

- Gift range chart

- Named-giving opportunities[3]

As you can see, although this may make sense for generating psychic benefits, it's not going to cut it with the impact buyer—such as the CEO I described in Chapter Seven. The impact buyer wants to know what you will do to solve his or her problem, not your statement of needs. The impact buyer needs a *compelling business case*.

Few organizations know how to craft a compelling business case, which is a proposition to an impact buyer to purchase outcomes. The substance of this business case is the substance of this book, so we need not recapitulate those concepts here. But the format and delivery of those concepts is worth elaborating. A strong business case needs only four elements:

1. *The need to buy:* the impact buyer's pain or desired goals
2. *The value proposition:* the direct benefits you can offer that address the impact buyer's needs
3. *Your strategy:* the activities or programs that will produce the benefits and the underlying theory of change (which explains why it will work)
4. *Your track record:* your key metrics and performance data that show your contribution and historical performance; this includes any testimonials

The presentation need not be more than ten slides. Of course, there is always a need for context, anecdotes, compelling images and a brief discussion of your organization's broader social impact. It is hard to make any case without those supporting elements—but they are *supporting* elements, not the core of the case. It's always a good idea to pressure test the business case with your first friend or internal champion, who can point out areas of weakness or language modifications for a particular impact buyer.

## Step 5: Overcome Channels of Resistance

When I was in the eighth grade, my parents signed me up for a judo class from a strict Korean instructor named Mr. Suk. I happened to be bigger than the other kids my age, so Mr. Suk paired me up with his son Joe, a brick wall of a kid who was also a national judo champion. Every day we sparred, and every day within seconds he'd flip me, trip me, or kick me to the ground. After enduring a week of this, I'd had about enough, and I went to my father to tell him I was done. He gave me some advice I'll never forget: "Jason, instead of letting Joe beat you every day, ask him to teach you the 'counters' to his moves—it'll make it much more interesting for him, too." It worked. Not only did I stay off the ground, but Joe taught me counters that I would never otherwise have learned, and I became a much better fighter.

Every one of us will encounter a Joe Suk when pitching to an impact buyer. It's not that people don't want to help, it's just a lot easier for them to say no. These are what I refer to as "channels of resistance" (a term I learned from my friend Tom Soma, executive director of Ronald McDonald House Charities of Oregon and Southwest Washington). The trick is to make them teach you the counters to overcome their own objections.

Judo and selling your impact have one thing in common: they both heavily depend on the concept of leverage. Leverage in judo means finding ways to turn the opponent's weight against him or her. It's the same thing in selling your impact: the goal is to locate your impact buyer's points of greatest need or desire and connect those to your work. In most cases, impact buyers object because you haven't established enough leverage. In some cases you may just be focused on the wrong stakeholder—such as someone who has no need to buy or ability to pay.

Here are some of the most common objections nonprofits hear when they are pitching their work to impact buyers:

- "I've never heard of your organization before."

- "That is important to us, but we can't afford it."

- "There are lots of people already doing that kind of work."

- "You need to talk to our charitable foundation."

- "Our department doesn't handle that."

- "We don't have bandwidth for that right now."

- "That doesn't fit our funding guidelines."

- "We don't have any budget for that right now; maybe next year."

In general, objections typically fall into one of three categories: you are not producing a high-enough value outcome (for the buyer); you are not articulating the value propositions compellingly; or you're running into logistical challenges (for example, timing, wrong budget, not the right decision maker). Here are some of the best counters—approaches you can use to overcome these objections:

- *Channel Joe Suk (turn your opponents into champions).*
  Ask your "opponent" what's missing or not resonating.
  It could be something relatively minor (such as
  logistical challenges) or it could be more significant
  (such as no true need to buy). One of my favorite lines
  is: "Help me convince you that you're wrong ... " It's a
  great way to turn a foe into a champion.

- *Sharpen your value proposition.* If your impact buyer isn't
  convinced, you're probably not being convincing
  enough. Find an internal champion who can help you
  learn more about what's really valuable to your
  prospect so you can zero in on the real pain or
  opportunity. Think of the old sales line: "You need to
  know your customer better than they know
  themselves."

- *Find a precedent, or a first friend.* If the buyer doesn't know you or hasn't partnered with someone like you before, find a way to lower the risk. Pointing to a precedent—another grant, another partnership, or another investment like yours—will help relieve that concern. So will a mutually respected first friend who can attest to your credibility and give confidence to your buyer.

- *Find a soft way to build a relationship.* Some organizations, particularly foundations, just take time to warm up. Rather than just waiting, you can find indirect or soft ways of deepening the relationship. Some suggestions: ask them to participate in a research project (not to fund it); collaborate with one of their current partners or grantees; invite a key employee to join an advisory board or speak on your panel at a conference; interview them for an article or white paper you're writing. The point is to establish some rapport and use that rapport to build trust and have the partner learn more about your work.

- *Make it a positive-sum transaction.* Some organizations really don't have any money, though they may highly value what you have to offer. This is particularly common with nonprofit or intermediary partners, even big ones like universities or hospitals. In these cases, there may be an opportunity to create a positive-sum transaction that is financially accretive for both parties. Sometimes twinning with an impact buyer to raise funds from a third party (for example, a government agency, foundation, or corporate partnership) will open the door to new funding that wasn't otherwise possible.

The things that work are the same things that we learned in high school: homework and practice are your best strategies. The more impact buyers you speak to, the more you will see what resonates and what doesn't, and the more creativity you will develop. Finally, remember that selling your impact is not about being slick or manipulative—it's about genuinely meeting other peoples' needs and creating value. If you do, your organization will effectively sell itself—all you have to do is point out the obvious.

# Chapter 9

# THE SEVEN IMMUTABLE LAWS
# OF SELLING YOUR IMPACT

I've offered a lot of advice in these pages, but if you take away just one set of "rules" or universal truths about selling your impact, these are the seven you should absolutely know.

1. *Go through the front door, not the back door.* Our inclination is usually to go to the corporate foundation rather than to the business, or to ask for the handout rather than the investment. Don't. Believe in the value you have to offer, and go through the front door to the key decision makers with a value proposition, not a philanthropic ask.

2. *Always use value pricing, not cost-plus.* Too often when we seek funding we ask for just enough money to cover our costs and then some. But selling your impact allows you to break free from this self-imposed asceticism. Value pricing is pricing based on the perceived value of your outcomes, not the actual cost of the program. Think about the Wal-Mart example we gave earlier: if you're generating $48 million in new spending for the company, would you rather base your proposal on the cost of your program or on a portion of the value you've created?

3. *Really know your customer (and speak their language).* Most of what we traditionally "know" about foundations or donors is

not likely to work in a selling-your-impact world. To create real leverage, you'll have to dig deep and use nontraditional sources of information to learn everything you can about your impact buyer—their economics, their pain, the social outcomes they value, and their actual "need to buy." And remember, you can have all the leverage in the world, but if people can't understand you, your message will fall on deaf ears!

4. *Sell painkillers, not vitamins.* This is one of the most valuable lessons I've ever learned. Particularly in the nonprofit sector, and particularly in a low-performing economy, people will buy only what they *have to have*, not what's nice to have. So make sure that your value propositions are not weak or too far out in the future to be perceived as real. Aim squarely at the pain of the impact buyer to create the maximum leverage. (This does not always have to be economic; sometimes you can address reputational, cultural, political, or even actual health-related pain.)

5. *Sell outcomes, not programs.* Always remember that buyers in the social capital market value the outcomes you can deliver, not your activities. This is a tough habit to break, because all of the conventions of fundraising today— including the case for support—are based on explaining what we do and how well we do it. When in doubt, just remember the "so what?" test—if you can't answer it, neither can your buyer.

6. *Don't oversell.* Selling isn't about "selling" or trying to manipulate; it's about solving other people's problems. No matter how rational your buyer or how much leverage you have, there must still be deference to the larger social purpose of your work. Go too far and you risk losing credibility. I recall one Fortune 500 CEO telling a nonprofit: "I don't want to hear about how you're going to help us sell more products—I

have an entire sales team for that—I want to hear about the good you do!" In another case, a nonprofit leader demanded a contribution from a large corporate partner, claiming, "You owe us!" It was a major turnoff, and he got nothing. It's a matter of finesse—and deference to the authentic social purpose of what this work is all about. That cannot be lost. As Janet Burton, program director at RMHC Global, pointed out: "Be confident in the value of the service you provide and the connection to the for-profit world *while you are achieving your mission*. Be grounded in your mission first. People still want charity to be charity. There's a fine line."

7. *Don't waste time on idiosyncratic funders*. There are over seventy thousand private foundations in the United States. Most will not qualify as impact buyers. Many are small family foundations that fund pet projects or fund through social connections. Even many of the big foundations (including a number of the top ten) focus on broad issue-areas like education or health and are not outcomes-driven. Remember, you can't create leverage without a need to buy. That said, more and more foundations are asking for outcomes, and that's a good thing. Just make sure that their interest in outcomes is bona fide and on the *front end* in terms of allocating resources, rather than on the *back end* as a compliance requirement.

Finally, remember that selling does not mean *selling out*. Selling your impact is not about forsaking your mission for others' personal gain. It is about *connecting* your social outcomes to the economic value of the market. There will be no value created without real social change. Your mission will always be paramount. But there is no reason why others who can derive value from the good work you do shouldn't also be sought after to finance it. If you do it right, tapping into the nearly unlimited resources of the social capital market will allow you to dramatically accelerate your mission and spend more time chasing outcomes than chasing dollars.

# Conclusion:
## Implications of the Social
## Capital Market

The social capital market has big implications for our work—new logic, new metrics, and new stakeholders—but does it really mean the *end of fundraising*? And what about grant makers, donors, and corporations—what does the social capital market mean for them?

Clearly, nonprofits still have to raise money. Of course, $300 billion of psychic money is nothing to waltz away from. Nor should we. This book does not advocate an end to fundraising so much as a renaissance. It posits a new, more hopeful approach to financing social good that draws from a greater source of strength, delivers a higher form of value, and is driven by our stakeholders' need to buy more than our need to sell. Selling our impact allows us to create greater leverage not only with new impact buyers but also with our existing stakeholders. Higher-value outcomes, a greater ability to articulate impact, and stronger selling skills will make our appeals that much more compelling to psychic beneficiaries, who may settle for a warm glow but really want a brilliant shine.

And though the social capital market may bring us more leverage, it also brings us more competition. We must contend with not only an increasing proliferation of nonprofits (a proliferation that we can expect to accelerate as social problems intensify) but also an increasing number of for-profit enterprises that are getting into the game of social change and aiming at the same outcomes. From eco-startups to social businesses, nonprofits and companies are increasingly competing for the same dollars in the social capital marketplace. Consider the U.S. Department of Commerce's i6 Challenge, which invites "entrepreneurs, investors, universities, foundations, and non-profits" to compete for millions of dollars aimed at innovative ideas that drive commercialization and entrepreneurship.[1] Competition in the social capital market is more intense than in the world of philanthropy, where collaboration is encouraged and comparisons are discouraged. To win, we're going to have to up our game, *really* innovate, and produce higher output for lower costs. That's no small feat.

To effectively compete for resources in the social capital market, nonprofits will need to be more intentional about the interplay between strategy and outcomes. One insight from the research behind this book is that the reason why it is so hard to quantify social impact is that, far too often, we are trying to measure outcomes that our programs are not designed to produce. Simply put, too many of us are trying to cantilever our way to the answer. When programs are specifically engineered to produce a particular outcome, they're pretty easy to measure. Think about how easy it is to measure whether a job training program reduces unemployment or whether a tutoring program increases grade advancement among those trained or tutored. Simple—both were designed to produce those outcomes, and the population is limited. But where we get into trouble is when we try to stretch our statements of impact beyond the outcomes that are reasonably proximate to our work. The market will keep us intellectually honest and make us more intentional about the way we design our programs.

Finally, the social capital market is expected to breed more innovation in how we finance our work. As we transcend the concept of the donation and forge more transactional relationships with impact buyers that have mutual consideration (legally), we open up to new funding mechanisms. The explosion of cause marketing is just one example. In 2009, companies were expected to spend $1.55 billion on cause partnerships.[2] Another example: nonprofits are generating revenues from social products and services that advance their mission. These revenues typically come from beneficiaries that can pay, which has proven to be an increasingly viable source of financing. Kickstart sells irrigation pumps to poor farmers. Kiva sells microloans. This new source of market-based financing is also yielding an unexpected positive social externality. According to a program officer at the Skoll Foundation, a funder of social entrepreneurs, "Our portfolio's innovations have shown us that when a beneficiary has to make a personal investment in something (purchasing eyeglasses, building and maintaining sanitation, paying for water distribution, etc.) they are far more likely to maintain and derive value from it than when something is given to them. Meaning, investment has a psychological value. Charity runs the risk of people not valuing things in the same way."[3] More market-based financing also promises a more controllable and stable revenue stream. In the future these streams might be securitized and sold, or borrowed against for working capital.

The social capital market also holds profound and unexpected implications for foundations and donors. For example, if the market is efficient in determining what nonprofits need to measure, foundations, high-net-worth donors, and venture philanthropists can step out of that role. Nonprofits themselves and their direct beneficiaries will have a much better idea of which measures are valuable and practical. Foundations and psychic donors may be in a better position to draft behind the market, and follow the metrics being set by more rational impact buyers. And this may also stimulate a new source of data for foundations and donors, who can look to actual market rewards as evidence of performance. This could come as a huge relief to nonprofits, which are often burdened by dozens of different measurement and "accountability" systems artificially created by dozens of different funders.

The social capital market may also free up capital for foundations and donors to invest more in general operations, capacity building, systemic innovation, and causes that may prove too difficult to finance otherwise. Many foundations and donors are frustrated by the limits of their own impact, increasingly running into a "boil the ocean" problem when it comes to funding direct service programs. There's simply never going to be enough philanthropic or government money to fund programs for everyone. This can offer a more meaningful, and measurable, role for philanthropy. The Bill and Melinda Gates Foundation, for example, has shifted more toward these systemic types of investments, creating inclusive markets for such things as malaria bed-nets and antiretroviral HIV drugs. The social capital market may also encourage foundations to redeploy their resources through program-related investments (PRIs) and other, more flexible financial instruments. According to the Gates Foundation: "Through tools like low-interest loans, guarantees, and investments in equity funds, the foundation will apply some of its resources to support enterprises and non-governmental organizations (NGOs) that are developing market-based solutions, seeding new innovations and helping ensure that critical solutions become sustainable and scalable in a manner that directly furthers the foundation's charitable purposes."[4] The Gates Foundation has committed $400 million to this pilot initiative.[5]

Clearly the social capital market has significant implications for corporations and the way they invest in social change. Because it is now OK to make an economic return from doing good, companies are increasingly looking at social change through the lens of their business rather than just through the lens of philanthropy. The opportunity for social innovation can attract much greater private investment in social impact goals—witness examples like GE's $6 billion investment in *healthymagination* and Vinod Khosla's $1-billion "green" venture capital fund. Companies are also increasingly focusing their core business on social outcomes as the gateways to business growth. For example, the European food giant Tesco has invested over $700 million in its strategy to enter the U.S. market by combating urban food deserts (neighborhoods devoid of quality grocers, where only high-sugar, high-fat, processed, and packaged foods are available). Tesco's Fresh & Easy Neighborhood markets have launched innovative products like "98 Cent Produce Packs" to make it less expensive for customers to eat fresh fruits and vegetables, and $8 family-sized prepared meals, which have proven to be top sellers.[6] We are still in the early stages of understanding the ways companies can offer social change. Nonprofits can also play a key role in educating business about the economic opportunities involved in addressing key social problems.

The social capital market offers our sector an incredible opportunity to breathe new wind into our sails and to chart a course for impact that takes us far beyond what we could ever have thought possible living off the occasional gusts of philanthropy. Like Columbus, we will only discover a new world once we set sail—but like America, the social capital market has been out there waiting for us all along.

# Epilogue: Frequently Asked Questions

*The End of Fundraising* promotes a new way of thinking about philanthropy and social change, which invariably raises a host of caveats and concerns. Through my discussions of these concepts with sector leaders, academics, MBA students, funders, and nonprofit executives, good questions have been raised. Here are some frequently asked questions and my responses.

**Q** Are you saying that we should stop pursuing traditional "feel good" donors?

**A** No. I believe that all donors are valuable, regardless of their motivations. Psychic donors and impact buyers are not an either/or proposition. This book does not advocate that we stop taking psychic dollars from our supporters, but rather that we include a new set of donors in our consideration set: impact buyers. Those that give to your organization because they emotionally respond to your mission are no less worthy than others—in fact, they may even be more valuable because of their loyalty! A recent survey found that 78 percent of all donors were 100 percent loyal, meaning that there is virtual certainty that they will give to the same organization again.[1] Donors are valuable assets, particularly for those organizations who have built large donor databases. What's more, many psychic donors can also *become* impact buyers if they learn about the impact your organization can have or how they could stand to benefit personally or institutionally.

Q Should we be concerned about corporations setting the social agenda? Isn't that dangerous?

A Indeed, we should be concerned about letting corporations dictate our social values, but this is not likely to happen. The approach I am suggesting is just the opposite—that we, nonprofits, set our own social agendas, and then find creative ways to connect our social outcomes to the needs of impact buyers. That's why in Part One we used our stakeholders to define our Success Equation and our outcomes first. The premise of the book is that positive social impact can create tremendous economic value, and that includes business benefits for corporations. There are several buffers to protect us against corporate social tyranny. First and foremost, the role of government is to regulate corporate behavior and step in when companies act in ways that are contrary to the public interest. Second, the growth of CSR watchdog groups and social activists has been tremendous, and they are a powerful force in holding companies accountable and exposing social and environmental injustices. Finally, consumers have enormous leverage, and they can exercise that leverage to reward companies for social outcomes that consumers value. Tesco will sell fresh fruits and vegetables in food deserts only if they are rewarded by consumers for doing so.

Q How do we guard against "selling out"? What if nonprofits pervert their missions just to chase the almighty dollar?

A The social capital market highlights the fine line between social good and greed. Why, for example, do we give a Nobel Prize to microlenders like Mohammed Yunus and an indictment to payday lenders? It will be up to society and policy makers to police the boundary between what is good and what is evil. But as with all good public policy, we must weigh the costs against the social benefits and come out in favor of those ideas and initiatives that are net positive. Moreover, the reality of the social capital market is that economic value is created through positive social change—by producing outcomes that, by virtue of their happening, produce economic and other market benefits. For example, retailers will benefit from increased SNAP spending only if we succeed in achieving the social outcome of registering more eligible families for the program. In this way, nonprofit incentives should be aligned with market incentives. There will certainly be some exceptions—for example, the nonprofit that promotes corporate products to its membership base simply for economic gain with no social consequence. Nonprofit boards will need to regulate against these ethical breaches, as they do already. In fact, the fiduciary duty of obedience—the lesser-known of three nonprofit board fiduciary duties (the other two are duty of care and duty of loyalty)—requires that board members be faithful to the organization's mission and not act in a way that is inconsistent with the goals of the organization.

Q Does this book apply better to some types of nonprofit than to others? It's easy to see how we can sell the impact of certain issues like environment, health, and economic development, but what about more generic youth services or health and human services?

A The concepts and tools in this book will apply to every nonprofit organization, regardless of mission or program type. This methodology is based on outcomes, not types of activities. One of the major limitations of our current approach to fundraising is that we see our work in terms of programs and activities to be funded or underwritten, rather than outcomes that can be valued and sold. To transition to this new way of thinking requires two steps: first, we must translate our activities into outcomes, and second, we must connect these social outcomes to impact buyers who can derive value from them. The concepts in this book teach you how to do this.

But once we do this, it becomes quite clear how charities that at first appear challenging to sell (such as arts, animal rights, children's health) can generate significant value for impact buyers. When I've seen organizations struggle with this approach, it has been related not to the nature of their work, but rather to the issues I identified in Chapter Six, Social Arbitrage: How to Increase Your Value (that is, it is a marketing or strategy problem).

Q What about some of the smaller nonprofits that are not able to produce high-value outcomes? Are they still candidates for this approach?

A Yes. Selling your impact is viable for both small and large nonprofits. In fact, many smaller nonprofits (charter schools and social entrepreneurs, to name a few) are using innovative strategies to produce extremely high value outcomes. However, there are many nonprofits, small and large, focused on a single activity or a fragment of an outcome (such as giving out a free meal or a suit for a job interview). These organizations can generate value in the social capital market, but they will need to reach for higher-value outcomes by extending their services or partnering with others. Given the fragmentation in the nonprofit sector, this may not be such a bad thing. Of course, organizations can always choose to subsist off of psychic support, and this may be the best approach for some nonprofits. In particular, there are many nonprofits that have no interest in producing higher-value outcomes. In 2009 the New York Times highlighted the fact that a growing number of single-purpose charities are continuing to win IRS approval, such as "a charity formed to ensure a 'chemical free' graduation party at a high school in Monticello, Minn.; two donkey rescue organizations; and two new chapters of the Sisters of Perpetual Indulgence, a group of cross-dressing 'nuns' who recently raised more than

$25,000 for AIDS treatment and other causes with an event featuring a live S-and-M show."[2]

Q  How did you identify the high-value outcomes? Why those three?

A  The three high-value outcomes (status change, ROI, and system change) discussed in Part Two, Marketing Your Impact, were identified from an analysis of the outcomes most frequently prioritized or supported by institutional funders (such as government, corporations, foundations, and funding intermediaries like United Way) with available outcomes data. Additional data was derived from dozens of interviews with corporate, foundation, and nonprofit leaders. These outcomes were then abstracted from their programmatic context and grouped into "like" categories to come up with the three classifications. The research methodology was similar to the approached I used to develop a common outcomes taxonomy for all nonprofits which has been published by the Urban Institute.[3]

Q  Won't this hurt capacity building or general operating support? If people just want to fund outcomes, then how will organizations cover their operating costs?

A  Selling your impact is about making decisions based on outcomes, not funding only programmatic work. If anything, value-driven funding allows for a much more flexible use of funds by nonprofits who are paid by impact buyers for what they produce, not how they produce it. Most of the dollars received by the organizations profiled in this book were not restricted. Moreover, as I mentioned in the Conclusion, the trends in the social capital market may point foundations more in the direction of support for nonprofit capacity building and innovation. The distinction made by foundations between "program-related" and "general operating" expenditures is a vestige of the independent sector, primarily designed for the purposes of accountability (to prove that dollars weren't being "wasted" on overhead and to allow for funders to claim some tangible impact). As the sector moves toward high-value outcomes and market-based funding, these distinctions will become increasingly irrelevant.

Q How do we know if our organization is ready to do this work?

A The one clear takeaway I've had from many years of work measuring impact is that measurement is more of a cultural than a conceptual or technical challenge. By this I mean that organizations that did not want to be outcomes-driven could not be outcomes-driven. Selling your impact requires a new mind-set and openness to thinking about your work in a very different way. It also requires staff buy-in and support. Leadership is critical to create a safe place in which conversations about selling your impact can take place and to incent the right behavior for change. But success is also a big culture-builder, and creating some initial "wins" with funders will help reify this idea for your staff and prove that change is possible and that there is a better way.

# Notes

*Preface*

1. "Money for Good: The U.S. Market for Impact Investment
   and Charitable Gifts from Individual Donors and Investors."
   Hope Consulting, May 2010. [http://www.hopeconsulting.us/
   pdf/Money%20for%20Good_Final.pdf.]

*Introduction*

1. "Food Stamp List Soars Past 35 Million." *Reuters*, September
   3, 2009. [http://www.reuters.com/article/
   idUSTRE5825OT20090903].

2. Fulton, K., and Blau, A. "Cultivating Change in
   Philanthropy." Monitor Group 2005.
   [http://www.futureofphilanthropy.org/files/workingpaper.pdf].

3. Ibid.

4. Leonhardt, David. "What Makes People Give?" *New York
   Times*, March 9, 2008. [http://www.nytimes.com/2008/
   03/09/magazine/09Psychology-t.html?pagewanted=2&_r=
   2&sq=karlan&st=nyt&scp=1].

5. "Fast Facts." National Center for Education Statistics, 2010.
   [http://nces.ed.gov/fastfacts/display.asp?id=372].

6. Colliver, V. "Preventative Health Plan May Prevent Cost
   Increases/Safeway Program Includes Hot Line, LifeStyle
   Advice." *San Francisco Chronicle*, February 11, 2007.
   [http://articles.sfgate.com/2007–02–11/business/
   17229896_1_safeway-s-ceo-health-care-steve-burd].

7. Cone, Inc. "Past. Present. Future. The 25th Anniversary of Cause Marketing," 2008. [http://www.coneinc.com/stuff/contentmgr/files/0/8ac1ce2f758c08eb226580a3b67d5617/files/cone25thcause.pdf]; Cone, Inc. "Cone Cause Evolution and Environmental Survey," 2007. [http://www.coneinc.com/files/2007ConeSurveyReport.pdf]; Cone, Inc., "2004 Corporate Citizenship Study," 2004. [http://www.coneinc.com/news/request.php?id=1086].

8. Ibid.

9. Ibid.

10. Kumar, J. S., and Sarangarajan, S. "SKS Microfinance IPO Attracts Strong Demand." *Wall Street Journal*, August 2, 2010. [http://online.wsj.com/article/NA_WSJ_PUB:SB10001424052748704271804575405223356063904.html].

11. Bellman, E. "IPO Pits Profit vs. Altruism." *Wall Street Journal*, July 9, 2010. [http://online.wsj.com/article/NA_WSJ_PUB:SB10001424052748703609004575355460120599280.html].

12. Cui, C. "For Money Managers, a Smarter Approach to Social Responsibility." *Wall Street Journal*, November 5, 2007. [http://online.wsj.com/article/SB119421532355881782.html?mod=todays_us_the_journal_report].

13. Ibid.

14. Middleton, D. "MBAs Seek Social Change." *Wall Street Journal*, October 15, 2009. [http://online.wsj.com/article/NA_WSJ_PUB:SB10001424052748704107204574469602649140462.html].

15. Dizik, A. "Executive Education: Schools, Firms Gauge Social Impact." *Wall Street Journal*, March 4, 2010. [http://online.wsj.com/article/NA_WSJ_PUB:SB10001424052748704541304575099692417734172.html].

16. Banchero, S. "Education Contest Yields 18 Finalists." *Wall Street Journal*, July 28, 2010. [http://online.wsj.com/article/

SB10001424052748703977004575393062887310840.html?
KEYWORDS=white+house+social+innovation].

17. Burton, T. "Hospitals Find Way to Make Care
    Cheaper—Make It Better." *Wall Street Journal*, October 8,
    2009.
    [http://online.wsj.com/article/SB125478721514066137.html].

18. "Understanding the LOHAS Lifestyle." *Conscious Ventures*,
    March 4, 2010. [http://consciousventures.com/tag/
    lohas-consumer-trends/].

19. Zolli, A. "Business 3.0." *Fast Company*, March 1, 2007.
    [http://www.fastcompany.com/magazine/113/open_fast50-
    essay.html?page=0%2C3].

20. "NMI Reveals Top Ten Trends of 2007." National
    Marketing Institute press release, March 1, 2007.
    [http://www.lohas.com/print/100120_print.html].

21. "GE's 2008 Ecomagination Revenues to Rise 21%, Cross $17
    Billion." General Electric press release, October 21, 2008.

22. "European SRI Study 2008." *Eurosif*, October 2008.
    [http://www.eurosif.org/publications/sri_studies].

23. Social Investment Forum. "Socially Responsible Investing
    Facts." [http://www.socialinvest.org/resources/
    sriguide/srifacts.cfm].

24. Ibid.

25. Ibid.

26. "European SRI Study 2008."

27. "Dow Jones Sustainability World Index, October 2009." *Dow
    Jones Sustainability Indexes*, 2009. [http://www.sustainability-
    index.com/djsi_pdf/publications/Factsheets/
    SAM_IndexesMonthly_DJSIWorld.pdf].

28. The Goldman Sachs Group, Inc. "Introducing GS Sustain,"
    June 22, 2007. [www.unglobalcompact.org/docs/summit2007/
    gs_esg_embargoed_until030707pdf.pdf].

29. http://www.hbs.edu/research/pdf/11-017.pdf.

30. Banjo, S. "New Investing Standards Coming for Microfinance." *Wall Street Journal* blogs, September 25, 2009. [http://blogs.wsj.com/financial-adviser/2009/09/25/new-investing-standards-coming-for-microfinance].

31. "Workers Want Ethical, Socially Responsible Companies, Survey Finds." *Workforce*, October 30, 2009. [http://www.workforce.com/section/00/article/26/77/05.php].

32. Cone, Inc. "Cone Cause Evolution and Environmental Survey," 2007. [http://www.coneinc.com/files/2007ConeSurveyReport.pdf].

33. "Service." [http://www.whitehouse.gov/issues/service].

34. Barnes, M. "The Social Innovation Fund: Government Doing Business Differently." The White House, July 22, 2010. [http://www.whitehouse.gov/blog/2010/07/22/social-innovation-fund-government-doing-business-differently].

35. http://www.whitehouse.gov/the-press-office/2010/09/22/remarks-president-millennium-development-goals-summit-new-york-new-york.

36. United States Department of Education. *Investing in Innovation*, October 2009. [http://www2.ed.gov/programs/innovation/factsheet.html].

37. "UN Climate Change Impact Report: Poor Will Suffer Most." Environment News Service, April 6, 2007. [http://www.ens-newswire.com/ens/apr2007/2007-04-06-01.asp].

38. "U.S. Charitable Giving Falls 3.6 Percent in 2009 to $303.75 Billion." The Center on Philanthropy at Indiana University, June 9, 2010. [http://www.philanthropy.iupui.edu/news/2010/06/pr-GUSA2010.aspx].

39. Giving USA Foundation, Giving USA, 2007.

40. Peschong, A. "LOHAS: The Next Secular Shift." *Seeking Alpha*, March 2, 2010. [http://seekingalpha.com/article/191393-lohas-the-next-secular-shift].

41. "Report: Socially Responsible Investing Assets in U.S. Surged 18 Percent from 2005 to 2007, Outpacing Broader Managed Assets." Social Investment Forum press release, March 5, 2008. [http://www.socialinvest.org/news/releases/pressrelease.cfm?id=108].

42. National Center for Education Statistics. "Fast Facts." 2010. [http://nces.ed.gov/fastfacts/display.asp?id=372].

43. U.S. Department of Health and Human Services, Center for Medicare and Medicaid Services. "National Health Expenditure Projections 2009–2019," 2009. [https://www.cms.gov/NationalHealthExpendData/downloads/proj2009.pdf].

44. This figure according to a corporate responsibility officer, December 4, 2008. [http://www.thecro.com/files/CROMedia%20Kit2009_MB.pdf]. Explanation provided by Jay Whitehead, president and publisher, CRO, based on a personal interview with Jason Saul conducted February 22, 2010: "This figure represents total spent on corporate responsibility, which includes environmental sustainability, governance, risk, compliance, social responsibility, and philanthropy; it was calculated by adding up the fees charged by about 450 service providers and 100 NGOs for sustainability, CSR, and philanthropy-related services and technologies in the U.S., Canada, and Western Europe."

45. Bush, G. W. South Carolina Republican debate, September 15, 2000.

46. Nichols, M. "Charities Mimic Wall Street to Woo Wealthy Donors." *Reuters*, July 1, 2010. [http://www.reuters.com/article/idUSTRE6603YB20100701?type=domesticNews].

47. Harold, J. "The Nonprofit Marketplace: Getting Social Impact Bang for Our Philanthropic Bucks." *Huffington Post*, February 13, 2009. [http://www.huffingtonpost.com/paul-brest/guest-post-jacob-harold_b_166840.html].

48. Macfarquhar, N. "Banks Making Big Profits from Tiny Loans." *New York Times*, April 13, 2010. [http://www.nytimes.com/2010/04/14/world/14microfinance.html].

49. http://www.ge.com/pdf/investors/events/05072009/ge_healthymagination_pr.pdf.

50. http://www.nytimes.com/2010/10/06/business/global/06khosla.html?_r=1.

51. Hall, J. "Too Many Ways to Divide Donations?" *Christian Science Monitor*, June 20, 2005. [http://www.csmonitor.com/2005/0620/p13s01-wmgn.html].

52. Data derived from the NTEE National Taxonomy of Exempt Entities.

53. "Charities Working to Prevent and Cure Breast Cancer." *Charity Navigator*, 2006. [http://www.charitynavigator.org/asset/_articles_/2006/breast_cancer_charities.pdf].

54. "Money for Good: The U.S. Market for Impact Investment and Charitable Gifts from Individual Donors and Investors." *Hope Consulting*, May 2010.

55. "The Effect of the Economy on the Nonprofit Sector: A June 2010 Survey." *Guidestar*, 2010. [http://www2.guidestar.org/rxg/news/publications/nonprofits-and-economy-june-2010.aspx?hq_e=el&hq_m=725434&hq_l=3&hq_v=2692359cf1].

56. Ibid.

57. Bellman, E. "IP Pits Profit vs. Altruism." *Wall Street Journal*, July 9, 2010. [http://online.wsj.com/article/NA_WSJ_PUB:SB10001424052748703609004575355460120599280.html].

58. McDonald's Corp. "Cause That Counts: Consumers Switch Brands to Support a Cause." [http://www.aboutm cdonalds.com/mcd/students/mcdonalds_does_good/ cause_that_counts.html].

59. "Social Return on Investment Collection." *RedF*, 2010. [http://www.redf.org/learn-from-redf/publications/119].

60. Ibid.

## Part I

1. Wilhelm, I. "Start-Ups of New Charities See No Slowdown in Bad Economy." *Philanthropy Journal*, April 18, 2010. [http://philanthropy.com/article/Great-Recession-Generates-M/65102/].

2. Strom, S. "Charities Rise, Costing U.S. Billion in Tax Breaks." *New York Times*, December 5, 2009. [http://www.nytimes.com/2009/12/06/us/06charity.html?_r=1 &adxnnl=1&adxnnlx=1283277661-W86XaxEyfuHfWq/rkxRt7Q].

3. Ibid.

4. Ibid.

## Chapter 1

1. Google search performed on July 25, 2010.

2. National Council of Nonprofits. "Ethics and Accountability in the Nonprofit Sector." [http://www.councilofnonprofits.org/resources/resources-topic/ethics-accountability].

3. Internal Revenue Service. "2009 Form 990—Significant Changes." February 15, 2010. [http://www.irs.gov/charities/article/0,,id=218938,00.html].

4. Ibid.

5. Ibid.

6. National Council of Nonprofits. "Ethics and Accountability in the Nonprofit Sector."

7. Maryland Nonprofits. "Standards for Excellence: An Ethics and Accountability Code for the Nonprofit Sector." [http://www.marylandnonprofits.org/html/standards/04_02.asp].

8. "Mixed Response Toward Grading System for Charities." YouGov press release, May 25, 2010. [http://www.yougov.co.uk/corporate/pdf/press-gradingSystemCharities.pdf].

9. "Money for Good," May 2010.

10. Ibid.

11. Charity Navigator. "How We Rate Charities." [http://www.charitynavigator.org/index.cfm?bay=content.view&cpid=35].

12. Ibid.

13. Ibid.

14. Better Business Bureau. "Standards for Charity Accountability." [http://www.bbb.org/us/Charity-Standards/].

15. Ibid.

16. Ibid.

17. Ibid.

18. GiveWell. "About GiveWell." [http://www.givewell.org/about].

19. GiveWell. "Developing-World Education (in-depth review)." [http://www.givewell.org/international/education/detail].

20. Mayr, U., Harbaugh, W. T., and Burghart, D. R. "Neural Responses to Taxation and Voluntary Giving Reveal Motives

for Charitable Donations." *Science*, June 15, 2007, *316*(5831), pp. 1622–1625.

21. Ibid.

22. Michael Greenberg, CEO of The Plastics Exchange. Personal interview, July 8, 2010.

## Chapter 2

1. United States General Accounting Office (GAO). "Performance Measurement and Evaluation: Definitions and Relationships" (GAO/GGD-98–26). Washington, D.C: Author. [http://www.gao.gov/special.pubs/gg98026.pdf].

2. Lerner, R. M., and others. "Findings from the First Wave of the 4-H Study of Positive Youth Development." *Journal of Early Adolescence*, February 2005, *25*(1), 17–71.

3. GAO, "Performance Measurement and Evaluation."

4. Activity. BusinessDictionary.com [http://www.businessdictionary.com/definition/activity.html].

5. Sawhill, J., and Williamson, D. "Measuring What Matters in Nonprofits." *McKinsey Quarterly*, May 2001. [https://www.mckinseyquarterly.com/ Measuring_what_matters_in_nonprofits_1053].

6. Ibid.

7. Ibid.

8. Ibid.

9. San Juan County Marine Resource Committee. "An Introduction to the Five-S Framework for Site Con servation." [http://www.sjcmrc.org/reports/ Conservation_Planning_Lite.pdf].

10. Tuan, M. "Measuring and/or Estimating Social Value Creation: Insights into Eight Integrated Cost Approaches." Bill and Melinda Gates Foundation, December 15, 2008.

[http://www.gatesfoundation.org/learning/documents/wwl-report-measuring-estimating-social-value-creation.pdf];
Tuan, M. "Profiles of Eight Integrated Cost Approaches To Measuring and/or Estimating Social Value Creation." Bill and Melinda Gates Foundation, December 15, 2008. [http://www.gatesfoundation.org/learning/Documents/WWL-profiles-eight-integrated-cost-approaches.pdf].

*Chapter 3*

1. Ronald McDonald House Charities. "Mission and Vision." [http://rmhc.org/who-we-are/mission-and-vision/].

2. Boys and Girl Clubs of America. "Mission." [http://www.bgca.org/whoweare/mission.asp].

3. Free The Children. "Our Mission." [http://www.freethechildren.com/aboutus/mission/].

4. Smithsonian. "Mission." [http://www.si.edu/about/mission.htm].

5. Toyota. "Chairman's Message," 2003. [http://www.toyota.co.jp/en/ir/library/annual/pdf/2003/chairmans_message_e.pdf].

6. Google. "Company Overview." [http://www.google.com/corporate/].

7. Microsoft. "Our Mission." [http://www.microsoft.com/about/en/us/default.aspx#values].

8. One of the studies cited found that "The relationship of patients' perceptions of patient centeredness with their health and efficiency of care was both statistically and clinically significant. Specifically, recovery was improved by 6 points on a 100-point scale; diagnostic tests and referrals were half as frequent if the visit was perceived to be patient centered." Stewart, M., and others. "The Impact of Patient-Centered Care on Outcomes." *Journal of Family Practice*, 2000, 49(9).

[http://www.jfponline.com/Pages.asp?AID=2601&issue=September_2000&UID=].

9. Keila Stovall. Personal interview conducted by Hillary Harnett, November 6, 2009.


*Part II*

1. Leverage. *The Oxford Pocket Dictionary of Current English.* Oxford: Oxford University Press, 2009. [http://www.encyclopedia.com/doc/1O999-leverage.html].

2. Sloane, Charles. "Donation." *The Catholic Encyclopedia*, vol. 5. New York: Robert Appleton Company, 1909. [http://www.newadvent.org/cathen/05117a.htm].

3. Consideration. *West's Encyclopedia of American Law*, 2nd ed. The Gale Group, Inc., 2008. [http://legal-dictionary.thefreedictionary.com/consideration].

4. Internal Revenue Service. "2009 Data Book." 2009. [http://www.irs.gov/pub/irs-soi/09databk.pdf].

5. Urban Institute. "NCCS Definitions." [[http://nccsdataweb.urban.org/PubApps/nteeSearch.php?gQry=all&codeType=NPC].

6. Kilmer, D., Meehan. W., and O'Flanagan, M. "Investing in Society: Why We Need a More Efficient Social Capital Market—and How We Can Get There." *Stanford Social Innovation Review*, Spring 2004. [http://www.ssireview.org/pdf/2004SP_feature_meehan.pdf].

7. "Barack Obama." OpenSecrets.org. [http://www.opensecrets.org/pres08/summary.php?cycle=2008&cid=N00009638]; "Expenditures Breakdown." OpenSecrets.org. [http://www.opensecrets.org/pres08/expend.php?cycle=2008&cid=N00009638]; "John McCain." OpenSecrets.org. [http://www.opensecrets.org/pres08/summary.

php?cycle=2008&cid=N00006424]; "Expenditures Breakdown." OpenSecrets.org. [http://www.opensecrets.org/pres08/expend.php?cycle=2008&cid=N00006424].

8. Fulton and Blau, "Looking Out for the Future," p. 6.

9. Ibid.

10. Value. BusinessDictionary.com. [http://www.businessdictionary.com/definition/value.html].

11. Leonhardt, "What Makes People Give?"

12. United States Census Bureau. *The Big Payoff: Educational Attainment and Synthetic Estimates of Work-Life Earnings.* July 2002. [http://www.census.gov/prod/2002pubs/p23–210.pdf].

13. Lev, B., Petrovits. C., and Radhakrishnan, S. "Is Doing Good Good for You? Yes, Charitable Contributions Enhance Revenue Growth." New York University Stern School of Business, August 2006. [http://pages.stern.nyu.edu/~blev/docs/IsDoingGoodGoodForYou.pdf].

14. "Sponsorship Spending Receded for the First Time in 2009." IEG press release, January 26, 2010. [http://www.sponsorship.com/About-IEG/Press-Room/Sponsorship-Spending-Receded-for-the-First-Time-in.aspx].

15. "The Coca-Cola Company: Using Source Protection Planning to Identify Source Vulnerabilities." Global Environmental Management Initiative. [http://www.gemi.org/water/coca-cola.htm].

16. Ibid.

17. Ibid.

18. Ibid.

19. United States Department of Education. "The American Recovery and Reinvestment Act of 2009: Saving and

Creating Jobs and Reforming Education." March 7, 2009. [http://www2.ed.gov/policy/gen/leg/recovery/implementation.html].

20. Cain Miller, C. "Venture Firm's 'Green' Funds Top $1 Billion." *New York Times*, August 31, 2009. [http://www.nytimes.com/2009/09/01/business/01khosla.html?_r=4].

*Chapter 4*

1. "Building Community Through the Arts." LISC Chicago. [http://www.lisc-chicago.org/display.aspx?pointer=3337.]

2. "About the First Book Marketplace." First Book Marketplace. [http://www.fbmarketplace.org/servlet/Page?template=about.]

3. Elkington, J., and Hartigan, P. *The Power of Unreasonable People: How Social Entrepreneurs Create Markets That Change the World*. Boston, Mass.: Harvard Business School Press, 2008.

4. Ibid.

5. Based on analysis of National Association of Children's Hospitals and Related Institutions (NACHRI) data and RMHC data, 2009.

6. Press Ganey is a provider of patient satisfaction surveys, management reports, and national comparative databases for the health care delivery system.

7. Jalonick, M. "Government Asks Retailers to Better Welcome Food Stamps." *Huffington Post*, May 19, 2010. [http://www.huffingtonpost.com/2010/05/20/food-stamps-welcome-here_n_582223.html]; "USDA Wants to Increase Food Stamp Participation." *American Agricultural Law Association Blog*, May 20, 2010. [http://www.agandfoodlaw.com/2010/05/usda-wants-to-increase-food-stamp.html].

8. "Money for Good: The U.S. Market for Impact Investment and Charitable Gifts from Individual Donors and Investors." *Hope Consulting*, May 2010. [http://www.hopeconsulting.us/pdf/Money%20for%20Good_Final.pdf].

9. Ibid.

10. Ibid.

11. Ibid.

12. Swibel, M. "Microfinance Fever." *Forbes*, December 13, 2007. [http://www.forbes.com/forbes/2008/0107/050.html].

13. Ibid.

14. Kiva.org. "Facts & History." [http://www.kiva.org/about/facts].

15. CGAP. "Global Estimates." [http://www.cgap.org/p/site/c/template.rc/1.11.1792/].

16. Kumar, J. S., and Sarangarajan, S. "SKS Microfinance IPO Attracts Strong Demand." *Wall Street Journal*, August 2, 2010. [http://online.wsj.com/article/NA_WSJ_PUB:SB10001424052748704271804575405223356063904.html].

17. Vander Ark, T. "Why Prizes?" X Prize Foundation, October 25, 2007. [http://www.xprize.org/blogs/tom-vander-ark/why-prizes].

18. X Prize Foundation. "What Is an X Prize?" [http://www.xprize.org/about/x-prizes].

19. X Prize Foundation. "Future X Prizes." [http://www.xprize.org/future-x-prizes].

20. Ibid.

21. Ibid.

22. Ibid.

23. "And the Winner Is ... " McKinsey & Company, 2009. [http://www.mckinsey.com/App_Media/Reports/SSO/And_the_winner_is.pdf].

24. Ibid.

25. "Social Financial Engineering: Britain's Government Tries a New Way to Finance Social Spending." *Economist*, March 23, 2010. [http://www.economist.com/node/15763214].

26. "Social Impact Bonds." Social Finance. [http://www.social finance.org.uk/services/index.php?page_ID=15].

27. "Social Finance Launches First Social Impact Bond." Social Finance. [http://www.socialfinance.org.uk/downloads/ Social%20Impact%20Bond%20March%2018_FINAL%20(2). pdf].

28. "Social Financial Engineering," *Economist*.

29. "Social Finance Launches First Social Impact Bond," Social Finance.

30. The Robin Hood Foundation. "Approach." [http://www.robinhood.org/approach/get-results/metrics.aspx].

31. America Pet Products Association. "Industry Statistics and Trends." [http://www.americanpetproducts.org/ press_industrytrends.asp].

32. Parvensky, J., and Perlman, J. "Denver Housing First Collaborative: Cost Benefit Analysis and Program Outcomes Report." Colorado Coalition for the Homeless, December 11, 2006. [http://www.shnny.org/documents/FinalDHFCCostStudy.pdf].

33. Clough, G. W. "Two Centennials for the Smithsonian." *Smithsonian*, April 2010. [http://www.smithsonianmag.com/arts-culture/From-the-Castle-Two-Centennials-for-Smithsonian.html].

34. Mayer, F. "Inside Minnesota's Booming Bike Economy." *Minnesota Business*. [http://www.minnesotabusiness.com/inside-minnesotas-booming-bike-economy].

35. Ibid.

36. "Quick Facts." The Aspen Institute Center for Business Education, *Beyond Grey Pinstripes* blog. [http://www.beyondgreypinstripes.org/rankings/trends.cfm].


*Chapter 5*

1. Mission Measurement Analysis, 2009.

2. Lampkin, L. M., Winkler, M. K., Kerlin, J., Hatry, H. P., Natenshon, D., Saul, J., Melkers, J., and Seshadri, A. "Building a Common Outcome Framework to Measure Nonprofit Performance" (research report). Urban Institute, December 1, 2006. [http://www.urban.org/publications/411404.html].

3. The Robin Hood Foundation. "Investors Report 2008." [http://www.robinhood.org/media/167973/2008_robinhood_investorsreport.pdf].

4. Kickstart. "Our 5 Step Process." [http://www.kickstart.org/what-we-do/impact/].

5. Gulati-Partee, G., and Ranghelli, L. "Strengthening Democracy, Increasing Opportunities: Impacts of Advocacy, Organizing, and Civic Engagement in the Northwest Region." National Committee for Responsive Philanthropy, September 2010.[http://www.ncrp.org/files/publications/gcip-nw_report_low_res.pdf].

6. http://www.omlf.org/wp-content/uploads/2010/04/state-of-the-city-2009_report_final_web1.pdf.

7. The Humane Society of the United States. "About Us: Overview." [http://www.humanesociety.org/about/overview/].

8. The Humane Society of the United States. "Rampant Animal Cruelty at California Slaughter Plant." January 30,

2008. [http://www.humanesociety.org/news/news/
2008/01/undercover_investigation_013008.html].

9.  Ibid.

10. Doering, C. "Humane Society Finds More Downer Cattle
    Abuse." *Reuters*, June 25, 2008.
    [http://www.reuters.com/article/idUSN2548579020080625].

11. Ibid.

12. Rowan, A. "The Power of Ideas: Perceptions of Animals Shift
    in Science and Society." The Humane Society of the United
    States, July 14, 2008. [http://www.hsus.org/
    animals_in_research/animals_in_research_news/
    andrew_rowan_science_071408.html].

13. E-mail correspondence with Beth Rosen, director of strategy
    and performance measurement at the Humane Society of the
    United States, January 31, 2008.

*Chapter 6*

1.  Cone, Inc. "Past. Present. Future. The 25th Anniversary of
    Cause Marketing," 2008. [http://www.coneinc.com/stuff/
    contentmgr/files/0/8ac1ce2f758c08eb226580a3b67d5617/files/
    cone25thcause.pdf].

2.  Ibid.

3.  Ibid.

4.  Ibid.

5.  Ibid.

6.  Council of Foundations. "Frequently Asked Questions"
    (originally quoted from a Wirthlin Report).
    [http://classic.cof.org/FAQDetail.cfm?ItemNumber=717].

7.  Goldsmith, S. *The Power of Social Innovation*. San Francisco:
    Jossey-Bass, 2010.

*Chapter 7*

1. Brock, D. "Focus on a Customer's Need to Buy, Not Your Need to Sell." *Eyes on Sales*, July 5, 2007. [http://www.eyesonsales.com/content/article/ focus_on_a_customers_need_to_buy_not_your_need_to_sell].

2. Ibid.

*Chapter 8*

1. Association of Fundraising Professionals. "FAQ: Case for Support and Case Statements." [http://www.afpnet.org/ ResourceCenter/ArticleDetail.cfm?ItemNumber=3351].

2. Seiler, T. *Developing Your Case for Support.* San Francisco: Jossey-Bass, 2001.

3. Association of Fundraising Professionals, "FAQ: Case for Support and Case Statements."

*Conclusion*

1. United States Economic Development Administration. "Bring Innovative Ideas to Market." [http://www.eda.gov/i6].

2. "Sponsorship Spending on Causes to Total $1.55 Billion This Year." IEG Sponsorship Report, July 27, 2009. [https://www.sponsorship.com/User/Login.aspx? ReturnUrl=/iegsr/2009/07/27/Sponsorship-Spending-On- Causes-To-Total-$1–55-Bill.aspx&Access=0 &Reason=NoUser].

3. Kimberly Dasher Tripp, program officer at the Skoll Foundation. Personal interview, August 27, 2010.

4. Bill and Melinda Gates Foundation. "Program-Related Investments: Leveraging Our Resources to Catalyze Broader Support for Our Mission." [http://www.gatesfoundation.org/about/Pages/program-related- investments-faq.aspx].

5. Ibid.

6. Duff, M. "Fresh & Easy Sales Jump in Tesco Turn Around." BNET, June 16, 2009. [http://www.bnet.com/blog/retail-business/fresh-easy-sales-jump-in-tesco-turn-around/1762].

*Epilogue: Frequently Asked Questions*

1. "Money for Good," Hope Consulting, p. 16 (Preface, note 1).

2. Strom, "Charities Rise, Costing U.S. Billions in Tax Breaks" (Part One, note 2).

3. Lampkin et al., "Building a Common Outcome Framework" (Chapter Five, note 2).

# Acknowledgments

The End of Fundraising was made possible by the many nonprofit, foundation, and corporate clients of my firm, Mission Measurement, who contributed to and "ground–truthed" many of the ideas in this book.

In particular, I want to thank the early believers and first friends, among them Ricardo Millett, a hero to the evaluation world and an early mentor and friend; Don Stewart, a legend in the field and a great intellectual sparring partner and friend; Jim Williams, Don Jackson, and Pat Jones of Easter Seals, who have been early adopters of and believers in my work since day one; my friends at the Center for Nonprofit Management at Northwestern's Kellogg School of Management, Liz Livingston Howard, Jane Hoffman, and Jennifer Paul, who provided the forum to incubate many of my early ideas; Janet Burton and Nicole Rubin at Ronald McDonald House Charities, who were among the first proponents and supporters of this work; Marc and Craig Kielburger and the staff at Free The Children and Me to We, who have been pioneers of this work and role models for the concepts in this book; Wendy DuBoe of United Way of Metropolitan Chicago, who helped me to bring my ideas to fruition; and the many hundreds of nonprofit leaders who attended my lectures, workshops, and webinars and helped me to refine and advance my thinking.

I also want to thank the amazing staff of Mission Measurement, who have helped to develop and apply these concepts in practice with amazing world-beating organizations. In particular I want to thank Kimberley Silver, who was an absolutely instrumental thought partner and co-contributor to much of this work, and

Wendy Lazar, whose vaunted research skills could locate any digital needle in an Internet haystack.

The project team for this book was world class. Special thanks to my old friend Vince Hyman, who provided keen insights about the sector as well as a deft editorial hand; Allison Brunner, who bought this book and first believed in it; and my agent, Carol Mann, who helped me manage the nearly impossible task of writing two books at the same time.

# Index

## A

Accountability: California's Nonprofit Integrity Act, 36; impact as demonstrated value, 44–46; importance in nonprofit sector, 19–20, 34–39; IRS Form 990 and, 35–36; measuring nonprofit's impact, 43; publishing hospital treatment results, 8–9; Sarbanes-Oxley Act of 2002 and, 36; showing value in, 31, 34–44; watchdogs of, 39–42

Activities: costs of solicitation, 80–82; focusing on, 53–54; outcomes vs., 50–54; valuing outcome, not, 51–52

Affinity, donor, 82, 83

Akula, Vikram, 6, 22

Allen, Barbara McFadden, 126

American Marketing Association, 87

Andreoni, James, 4–5

Arts: demonstrating outcomes of, 110; developing patrons for, 101–102, 110, 113–114; finding primary consumers of impact in, 93–94; leveraging services linked to social change, 92

Association of Fundraising Professionals (AFP), 166–167

## B

BBB Wise Giving Alliance, 19, 40–41

Becerra, Xavier, 30

*Benchmarking for Nonprofits* (Saul), 34

Beneficiaries that can pay, 99–102; about, 99; finding, 114; Hyde Park Art Center, 101–102, 110; Kickstart, 100; microfinance and,

99–100; valuing organizations with positive outcomes, 101

*Big Payoff, The* (U.S. Census Bureau), 84

Bill and Melinda Gates Foundation, 57, 86, 180

Blau, Andrew, 82–83

Bloomberg, 11

BOP (bottom of the pyramid), 15

Boys and Girls Clubs of America, 59, 77–78

Boys Totem Town, 111

Branson, Richard, 86

Bridgespan Group, 18

Burton, Janet, 67, 175

Bush, George W., 18

BusinessDictionary.com, 50, 83

Businesses: adopting social responsibility, 6–7, 11–12; approaching decision makers in, 173; bringing nonprofits into world of, 23; building around social cause, 7; champions inside, 162–165; engaging as corporate partners, 95–99; finding their need to buy, 149–154; identifying key influencers on, 152; interest in social change, 9–10; key social issues in success of, 12–16; locating project money, 165–166; making case for funding support, 166–168; mission statements of, 59–60; overcoming resistance of, 168–172; performing social audits, 7–8; relationships with, 171; setting social agenda, 184; social issues becoming issues for, 5–6; speaking language of, 136, 173–174. *See also* corporate partners